Wage Flexibility and Unemployment Dynamics in Regional Labor Markets

Thomas Hyclak
Lehigh University

Geraint Johnes
University of Lancaster

1992

W.E. UPJOHN INSTITUTE for Employment Research
Kalamazoo, Michigan

Library of Congress Cataloging-in-Publication Data

Hyclak, Thomas.
    Wage flexibility and unemployment in regional labor markets /
Thomas Hyclak, Geraint Johnes.
      p.   cm.
    Includes bibliographical references (p.   ) and index.
    ISBN 0-88099-120-8 (pbk. : acid-free)
     1. Wages—United States. 2. Unemployment—United States.
3. Labor supply—United States—Regional disparities.   I. Johnes.
Geraint, 1958-   . II. Title.
HD475.H93   1992
331.1'0973—dc20

                                                         92-5782
                                                          CIP

Acknowledgements

This project has benefitted greatly from the comments and suggestions of many people. We wish to thank Neil Manning, Jim Taylor, Jon Innes, Larry Taylor, David Jones, Tony O'Brien and the participants at seminars at SUNY in Binghamton, Glasgow, Surrey, Cambridge and Lisbon. The careful reviews of earlier drafts of this book by Tim Bartik and two anonymous referees greatly improved the final product.

Quinghui Zhao and Jon Kramer provided excellent research assistance and Diane Oechsle deftly managed the arduous task of turning drafts into a finished book. We sincerely thank them for their contribution to this effort.

We are grateful to the Upjohn Institute for their financial support.

We dedicate this book to Jean and Jill.

The Authors

Thomas Hyclak received his Ph.D. in economics from the University of Notre Dame in 1976. He served as Assistant Professor of Economics at Ball State University before joining Lehigh University in 1979. He is currently Professor of Economics at Lehigh. Professor Hyclak has published articles on regional labor markets, the economic effects of trade unions and earnings differentials in the *Review of Economics and Statistics,* the *Industrial and Labor Relations Review,* the *Journal of Regional Science* and *Regional Studies,* among others. He is the co-editor of *Canada at the Crossroads* (JAI Press 1988) and *Economic Aspects of Regional Trading Arrangements* (New York University Press 1989).

Geraint Johnes received his Ph.D. in economics from Lancaster University in 1987. He has been lecturer in Economics at Lancaster University since 1982 and Visiting Professor of Economics at Lehigh University on a number of occasions. Dr. Johnes has published articles on regional economics, public finance, the economics of education and labor economics in the *Economic Journal, Oxford Economic Papers, Regional Studies* and the *Journal of Regional Science,* among others. He is the author of *Economics for Managers* (Prentice Hall 1990) and *The Economics of Education* (MacMillan 1993). He has been editor of the *International Journal of Manpower* and will be the editor of the new journal, *Education Economics,* beginning in 1993.

Contents

Tables

Figures

1

Introduction

Periods of high unemployment are generally accompanied by intensive economic research into the causes of and potential cures for unemployment. This was certainly the case during the decade of the 1980s, which witnessed a sharp increase in the number of empirical and theoretical analyses focused on labor market behavior in general and unemployment in particular. The research was motivated by both macroeconomic and regional unemployment issues.

The marked rise and stubborn persistence of the unemployment rate in most European countries during the 1980s led to renewed macroeconomic interest in the performance of aggregate labor markets. This literature has been intensively surveyed by Klau and Mittelstadt (1986), Helliwell (1988), and Gordon (1990a). The problem of unemployment persistence led most empirical and theoretical studies to focus on the question of wage rigidity, since persistent unemployment implies the failure of the self-correcting properties of wage adjustment. While the concept of wage rigidity has long played a central role in both classical (Pigou 1913) and Keynesian (Keynes 1936) theories of unemployment, recent efforts have been directed at explaining how wage rigidity and labor market disequilibria can result from the profit- and utility-maximizing behavior of firms and workers (Davidson 1990).

There are two major policy issues in this macroeconomic research. The first is the debate over the ability of expansionary monetary and fiscal policy significantly to lower the unemployment rate (Pierre 1984). The second policy question concerns the appropriate microeconomic policy to minimize the degree of wage rigidity and labor market disequilibria. There is evidence that wage rigidity differs across countries (Coe 1985), that those countries with less rigidity also had less serious unemployment problems in the 1980s (Grubb, Jackman, and Layard

1

1983), and that wage rigidity appears to be related to labor market policy and industrial relations differences across countries (Layard, Nickell, and Jackman 1991).

The regional problem motivating recent labor market research was the emergence of substantial diversity in U.S. regional economic performance during the 1980s. This diversity is illustrated by references in the popular press to the shift of economic activity from the "Rust Belt" to the "Sun Belt"; the effects of defense spending and high technology industries on the "Massachusetts Miracle," and the coexistence of "coastal" recovery with "heartland" recession. A number of studies have examined the causes of regional shifts in economic activity and the consequences of such shifts for unemployment, employment growth, and income prospects in various regions (see Markusen 1985; Clark, Gertler and Whiteman 1986; Lampe 1988; and Rodwin and Sazanami 1989). The policy issues connected to this research concern the appropriate adjustment policies to ameliorate the labor market consequences of regional change and the development strategies likely to succeed in an environment of regional change.

Thus far there have been relatively few attempts to apply the insights from aggregate labor market research to the analysis of regional unemployment. That is our focus in this book. We explore the extent to which wage rigidity differs across regional labor markets in the United States, the way in which wage rigidity affects the unemployment response to shifts in regional aggregate demand, and the determinants of differences in wage rigidity across regional labor markets. Our intent is to provide greater empirical content for the various theoretical models of wage rigidity, to enhance our understanding of the interaction of wage responsiveness and regional unemployment over the business cycle, and to provide some insight for state government policymakers who have been forced to assume greater responsibility for the design and execution of labor market policy (Leigh 1989).

Wage Rigidity and Unemployment

We can begin to analyze the relationship between wage rigidity and unemployment with the simple textbook supply and demand model of the aggregate labor market used by Kniesner and Goldsmith (1987). The aim of their review article is to present some stylized facts about the cyclical behavior of labor market aggregates and to compare the way in which various theories perform relative to these facts. There are four such facts that prove essential to describing how the aggregate U.S. labor market behaves in a "typical" post-World War II recession.

(1) The fall in real GNP during a recession is accompanied by a drop in employment of similar magnitude and a rise in the unemployment rate. The unemployment rate rises by about ⅓ of a point for every percentage point difference between trend growth in real GNP and actual real GNP growth. This relationship between unemployment and the real GNP gap is commonly referred to as Okun's law and is one of the most consistent empirical relationships observed in macroeconomic analysis.

(2) The rise in unemployment during a recession is largely due to new firings and layoffs and represents a decrease in the number of workers with jobs. Empirically, decreases in employment are far more important than reductions in hours worked in explaining the decrease in labor inputs used during a cyclical downturn.

(3) The aggregate real wage does not decline in the face of rising unemployment during a recession. The real wage is statistically independent of the level of economic activity as measured by real GNP.

(4) The aggregate labor supply curve appears to be relatively inelastic with respect to the real wage level. Thus a decrease in labor demand coupled with rigid wages leads to disequilibrium in the labor market rather than, as some have argued, a movement along a flat labor supply curve to a lower equilibrium level of employment at which any unemployment would be voluntary.

Figure 1.1 illustrates these stylized facts in a simple supply and demand model of the aggregate labor market during a recession. The immediate cause of a rise in unemployment is the decrease in labor demand associated with falling aggregate output. However, the role of wage rigidity in explaining unemployment is immediately clear. If the labor market operated in auction-market fashion and any excess supply put immediate downward pressure on the real wage, then the effect of

Figure 1.1 **Stylized Model of the Aggregate Labor Market in a Typical Post-World War II U.S. Recession.**

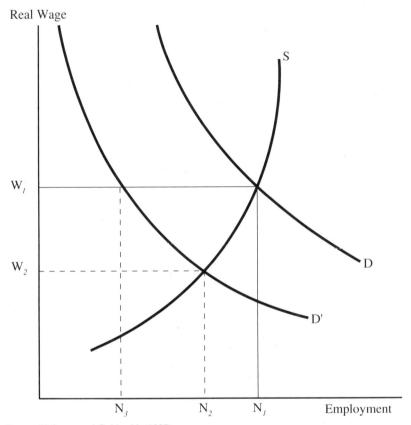

Source: Kniesner and Goldsmith (1987)

the decline in labor demand on total employment, and therefore in the unemployment rate, would be much less pronounced. The level of employment in figure 1.1 would fall only from N1 to N2 instead of to N3, if the real wage fell so as to clear the market. Real wage rigidity also plays a prominent role in explaining unemployment persistence. If labor demand remains depressed for several time periods and the real wage moves slowly if at all to the market-clearing level, then the time series data on the unemployment rate will exhibit persistence—a rise in unemployment in one period will not be offset by a fall in subsequent periods because the automatic adjustment mechanism in the market fails to work properly.

The analysis in figure 1.1 follows the usual textbook convention of treating labor demand and supply as determined by the real wage level in the absence of money illusion. Hence the importance of rigid real wages for the explanation of unemployment. However, the real wage is not determined in the labor market alone. Instead, labor market forces influence the money wage while the average price level reflects product market factors. Therefore, it is necessary to distinguish between nominal and real wage rigidity, which may differ in a given labor market. Our analysis focuses on the responsiveness of wage inflation to unemployment holding constant expectations about consumer price inflation. Hence, our concern throughout is with measuring and explaining regional differences in real wage rigidity.

Kniesner and Goldsmith's (1987) analysis of cyclical unemployment emphasizes the role of labor demand shifts resulting from decreased real output. Labor supply is passive in Figure 1.1, merely determining the number unemployed at any given level of demand and fixed real wage. In a regional labor market setting, however, it is possible that labor supply changes through net migration would play a more significant role in determining the unemployment rate and its persistence. However, recent studies by Topel (1986), Bartik (1991), and Holzer (1991) all conclude that shifts in labor demand dominate short-run movements in wages and employment in regional labor markets with significant mobility costs greatly lengthening the time span of labor supply adjustments through migration. In terms of figure 1.1, this means that a decrease in labor demand stemming from an economywide decrease in total spending – for example, the effects of monetary policy in the 1982 recession – would, in the short run, be treated in a similar way as a decrease in the demand for the goods of one region – for example, the effects of the fall in world oil prices in the 1986–87 recession in the "oil patch" states.

Our reading of the literature comparing aggregate labor market performance across countries leads us to add three additional stylized facts to the list provided by Kniesner and Goldsmith. There is some empirical evidence that the results of these international comparisons also apply to contrasts among regions within countries. The additional stylized facts are:

(1) Unemployment persistence appears to be virtually ubiquitous. In a careful study of some 19 countries, Robert Barro (1988, p. 34) found that "the general picture is one of high persistence of unemployment in the post-World War II period." He measured persistence by the AR1 coefficients in a time series analysis of unemployment rates. These coefficients lie close to unity for all countries in his sample bar Sweden, indicating the general lack of a tendency for unemployment to revert to a long-run mean.

(2) Wage flexibility varies across countries and regions in a manner that is correlated with differences in unemployment trends. Evidence on international differences in the responsiveness of wages to labor market disequilibrium is provided by Coe (1985 and 1988), Grubb, Jackman and Layard (1983), Grubb (1986), and Klau and Mittelstadt (1986). The latter three studies also provide results indicating that measures of wage rigidity are positively correlated with the change in unemployment from the 1970s to the 1980s across countries. The conclusion generally drawn from this type of analysis is that wage rigidity serves to exacerbate the unemployment consequences of macroeconomic shocks.

(3) Wage rigidity and unemployment persistence appear to be related to government labor market policy and the system of industrial relations. Barro (1988) finds that his measure of unemployment persistence is higher in countries with greater union density but lower in those countries where collective bargaining takes place in a centralized fashion. Layard, Nickell and Jackman (1991) find a similar result and add that generous unemployment compensation policies also contribute to unemployment persistence. On the other hand, Chan-Lee, Coe and Prywes (1987) find no evidence that wage responsiveness has been affected by changes in government labor policy. In general, research into the causes of wage induration has remained largely at the theoretical level to date.

While these three stylized facts are drawn from comparative studies of national differences in labor market performance, there is some

Table 1.1 **Measures of Unemployment Persistence and Wage Flexibility for 10 U.S. States and 11 West German Länder**

Area	Unemployment Persistence	Wage Flexibility
California	.9971	.6301
Florida	1.0000	.4392
Illinois	1.0426	.7490
Massachusetts	.9888	.2470
Michigan	1.0038	.4667
New Jersey	1.0014	.0228
New York	1.0138	.2719
Ohio	1.0062	.5408
Pennsylvania	1.0120	.7997
Texas	1.0167	.9188
Schleswig-Holstein	1.0537	.4090
Hamburg	1.0016	.5272
Niedersachsen	1.0586	.3601
Bremen	1.0654	.1826
Nordrhein-Westfalen	1.0499	.3202
Hessen	.9988	.5036
Rheinland Pfalz	1.0324	.4750
Baden-Würtemberg	.8970	.6216
Bayern	1.0472	.6148
Saarland	1.0575	.3144
West Berlin	1.0496	.3054

Source: Author's estimates. Unemployment persistence is the AR1 coefficient in an ARMA(1,1) time series analysis of the log of the unemployment rate from 1971 to 1985. Wage Flexibility is the unemployment rate coefficient in a Phillips curve regression explaining wage inflation estimated over the 1971 to 1985 period, as reported in Hyclak and Johnes (1989).

preliminary evidence to suggest that they also apply to regional differences as well. In table 1.1 we provide some statistics regarding the applicability of the first two of these stylized facts to regional analysis. For comparative purposes the table lists data on unemployment persistence and wage flexibility for the ten most populous U.S. states and the 11 Länder in West Germany.

In the first column are indexes of unemployment persistence calculated as in Barro (1988) from a time series analysis of the logarithm of regional unemployment rates over the 1971–1985 period. The indexes are the AR1 coefficient derived from treating the unemployment time series as an ARMA(1,1) process. Values of the coefficient close to unity suggest a high degree of persistence. It is clear from even a cursory examination of the data that unemployment persistence is a common characteristic of regional as well as national labor markets.

In the second column, we present measures of wage responsiveness drawn from our study of regional Phillips curves in Europe and the U.S. (Hyclak and Johnes 1989). These measures are the absolute coefficients of the current unemployment rate in regressions explaining wage inflation as function of the unemployment rate and expected consumer price inflation over the 1971–1985 period. As is clear from the table, there is a considerable degree of variation in this measure of wage responsiveness across the regions within each country. This is not an unusual finding. Studies of regional Phillips curve regressions by Kaun and Spiro (1970), Mathur (1976) and Blackley (1989), among many others, all show differences across regions in the estimated response of wage inflation to unemployment.

In our previous papers (Hyclak and Johnes 1989 and Johnes and Hyclak 1989) we report regression results showing a positive relationship between wage rigidity and unemployment trends across regions in Europe and the United States. Thus, like the findings regarding international differences, it seems possible to conclude that wage rigidity heightens the regional unemployment response to macroeconomic shocks. Finally, Kaun and Spiro (1970) and Hyclak and Johnes (1992) present evidence indicating that wages may be more flexible in regions with lower rates of unionization. These results suggest that wage rigidity differences are a potentially important determinant of regional differences in labor market performance. This book presents the results of a comprehensive empirical examination of this issue concentrating on the U.S. states.

Theories of Wage Inflexibility

The studies discussed above have served to establish the existence and importance of both unemployment persistence and wage rigidity. They do not, however, help us fully identify the reasons why such imperfections exist in the labor market. An understanding of these reasons is essential if governments are to take the appropriate policy steps to remove these sources of unemployment. Fortunately, the last decade or so has witnessed the development of several important theoretical approaches to explaining the existence of persistent unemployment and wage inflexibility. Useful full-length surveys of these have been conducted by Carruth and Oswald (1987), Davidson (1990), and Nickell (1990). Here we consider only the theories which have generated most interest amongst economists. These can usefully be classified into two groups. The first of these concerns factors which arise from the interaction of firms and their employees. The second concerns policy issues.

Consider first the sources of wage inflexibility which might arise from the manner in which employers and employees bargain. These rationalizations all rely on the idea that wage rigidity confers a benefit, since it enables some sort of (assumed) cost within the employment relationship to be bypassed. This bypassed cost might, for instance, be the disutility imposed by excessive risk, or it could be the cost of monitoring worker effort and co-operation, or it could be the costs associated with hiring, firing and training staff.

The theory of implicit contracts (Baily 1974; Azariadis 1975) is based on voluntary agreements entered into by firms and workers. These agreements guarantee risk-averse workers a degree of income stability in return for wages somewhat below the average (over the cycle) of the marginal revenue product. Both firms and tenured workers gain from these contracts; firms gain because their total labor cost falls, while tenured workers gain because they face a less risky environment. A slump causes unemployment because the real wage rises as product prices fall, thereby pricing untenured workers out of jobs. In this model, then, nominal wage inflexibility reduces the costs associated with workers' risk. The success of the contracts model in explaining unemployment relies critically on the failure of indexation (or cost-of-living adjustments) fully to maintain the real wage at market-clearing level (Schultze 1985). Sure enough, wages are not fully indexed in the world; but without a good theoretical reason for this observed fact, contract theory remains unsatisfactory.

A theory of more recent vintage, closely related to that of implicit contracts, has been proposed by Lindbeck and Snower (1988). This is the theory of insiders and outsiders. Insiders are currently employed or temporarily laid-off workers, while outsiders are unemployed workers whose bargaining power with the representative firm is limited. The externality in this case takes the form of turnover costs (due to hiring and training). These enable insiders to extract a rent from their employers, who are willing to pay a premium to prevent quits. Insiders can increase this rent by issuing credible threats to harass any outsiders who are hired, thereby further reducing the productivity of new recruits. Thus the insiders can prevent outsiders from pricing themselves into work by adopting limit pricing behavior in their wage bargaining.

The insider-outsider categorization of workers into two distinct groups is reminiscent of earlier theories which explained the low degree of wage responsiveness to external conditions by appealing to institutional arguments. Chief amongst these is Doeringer and Piore's (1971) theory of internal labor markets. In their model, many posts within a firm are filled by promotion from within. The remuneration associated with these posts is not, therefore, determined by competitive forces in the labor market, since open competition for these jobs is absent. While the theory of internal labor markets is often advocated as an alternative to the dominant neoclassical paradigm, it is consistent with a neoclassical world in which the costs of assessing external (or secondary) labor market candidates for promoted positions is high relative to the costs of monitoring internal applicants. The challenge now faced by advocates of both the insider-outsider and internal labor market theories is to explain how some workers become insiders while others do not.

A further explanation of wage rigidity is provided by the theory of efficiency wages (Lazear 1981; Summers 1988). The central idea is that worker motivation and productivity depend positively on the level of wages. Consequently, firms are reluctant to lower wages during a downturn, since this might result in a drop in worker effort and firm profitability. The cost bypassed by the stickiness of wages in this instance is the potential detrimental effect on output of reduced worker effort. The ease of modeling afforded by the efficiency wage idea is appealing, but the theory has faced a number of criticisms. Most seriously, the wage in such models performs two tasks – it regulates the supply of both hours and effort. The realism of the model may be enhanced by reinstating the missing price; in other words, we can introduce into the remuneration system a productivity bonus (or a promotion structure, or an equity ownership scheme). Once this is done, the theory is no longer able to explain unemployment. Efficiency wage theory can, therefore, satisfactorily explain unemployment only where incentive schemes are, for rational reasons, absent.

Consider now the second broad class of variables which might influence wage flexibility. These are variables which may more easily be subject to policy influence. The first of these potential determinants of wage viscosity is unemployment compensation. Burtless (1987) argues that unemployment benefits increase the duration of unemployment by financing job search and raising the reservation wage of the unemployed. Benefits may also cushion the detrimental effects of short-term unemployment and may therefore raise the equilibrium wage which falls out of an efficiency wage model. By providing a floor below which wages in an otherwise competitive nonunion sector cannot fall, benefits can further exacerbate unemployment (Minford *et al.* 1985). Further, benefits may tilt union preferences away from a concern about their members' employment prospects and towards the achievement of higher wage levels.

Minimum wage legislation imposes a floor below which the wage may not fall. This institutional rigidity is obviously capable of causing unemployment, although its empirical importance as a source of market failure in the United States is likely to be slight (Chan-Lee, Coe and Prywes 1987). The minimum wage rate is rarely changed, so its real value is constantly being eroded; furthermore, relatively few workers are covered by the minimum wage.

Finally, the impact of trade union behavior on the flexibility of wages has been a subject of much debate. The efficient bargains model of McDonald and Solow (1981) shows that union and firm negotiations over employment and wage levels can lead to Pareto optima characterized by wage inflexibility and unemployment. Although Clark (1990) finds that this result does not extend to the more realistic case of bargains struck over wages and the worker-to-machine ratio, union behavior remains an important potential source of nominal rigidity (Minford *et al.* 1985). We shall therefore pay special attention to the role of unions, and, in particular, the effects of the right-to-work laws adopted by some states.

Aims and Methodology

It should be clear from the above that we have available at this stage a number of alternative theories of wage inflexibility, each of which remains to be fully developed. Unfortunately, while theory has been racing ahead, empirical work on this issue remains relatively underdeveloped. Empirical analysis can throw light on which of the alternative theoretical research programs is most likely to bear fruit, and at the same time can allow important policy conclusions to be drawn. It is with this in mind that we embarked upon the present study. Specifically, we wanted to use empirical methods to answer the following questions:

(1) What local and regional patterns can be observed in labor market behavior in the United States?
(2) What are the determinants of wage inflexibility?

These questions have not until now been seriously addressed in the empirical literature, but their answers are critically important. Indeed, the second question addresses one of the major unsolved macroeconomic puzzles. Both questions are of obvious policy relevance; this being so, our results can provide information about the impact on wage flexibility and unemployment of:

- right-to-work legislation
- policies to encourage the development of small firms
- minimum wage policy
- unemployment benefits.

In addition, we provide evidence about the impact of industry mix and other structural indicators upon wage flexibility. The main theoretical approaches to involuntary unemployment are confronted with the data in order to establish which avenues offer the most promise for future work.

In answering the key questions, we use a unified framework built upon a simple two-equation model of the labor market. The first equation is a traditional expectations-augmented Phillips curve, where the rate of wage inflation is determined by unemployment and by the expected rate of price inflation. The theory underlying this equation has been explained by Friedman (1968) as follows. Starting from a point of equilibrium,

> suppose that . . . the authority increases the rate of monetary growth. This will . . . tend initially to lower interest rates and . . . income and spending will start to rise. To begin with much or most of the rise in income will take the form of an increase in output and employment . . . Producers will tend to react to the initial expansion in aggregate demand by increasing output, employees by working longer hours, and the unemployed by taking jobs now offered at former nominal wages . . . There is always a temporary trade-off between inflation and unemployment . . . The temporary trade-off comes from unanticipated inflation (pp. 9–10).

The Phillips curve is thus a close relative of the aggregate supply curve (Lucas 1973; Sargent and Wallace 1975), since it concerns a supply-side response to errors in the formation of price expectations.

The long-run responsiveness of wage changes to the rate of unemployment, as measured by the appropriate Phillips curve coefficient, may be used as a measure of real wage flexibility (Grubb, Jackman and Layard 1983; Coe 1985; Hyclak and Johnes 1989; Johnes and Hyclak 1989). This aspect of our Phillips curve results therefore merits considerable attention in the present context, since it enables us to analyze the magnitude and nature of wage viscosity for each of the geographical samples in the study.

This tells only half a story, though. Certainly unemployment exerts an influence upon wage inflation. But the rate of change of wage rates also has an impact on unemployment. This is because the derived demand for labor varies negatively with the real wage. Consequently, any increase in wages that is not matched by an increase in prices or product market demand must lead to a decline in the demand for labor, and unemployment results. This idea was put forward by Irving Fisher (1926) and can be derived from Okun's law (Okun 1962). To be more precise, we model the unemployment rate as a function of lagged unemployment, nominal growth of aggregate demand, and wage inflation. This specification of the "Fisher curve" allows us to investigate certain issues concerning unemployment persistence, since the coefficient on the lagged dependent variable captures an effect similar (though not identical) to Barro's persistence measure.

In order fully to account for the simultaneous nature of the relationship between wage inflation and unemployment, we use a systems method to estimate the parameters of both the Phillips curve and the Fisher curve. This approach is one of the major innovations we introduce in chapter 2. The second innovation introduced in that chapter concerns the level of analysis at which our analyses are conducted. Following the lead of Blackley (1989), we study data at state level within the United States; our study, however, improves upon earlier work in that we cover all 48 contiguous states. Moreover, our disaggregation goes further than state level, for we also present estimates of the model for 16 of the largest standard metropolitan areas.

Our reasons for disaggregating the analysis to state and metropolitan areas are several. First and foremost, we disaggregate because labor market decisions are typically reached at the local level. In a full employment world, migration might be expected to equalize remuneration for given work across localities, thus removing in the long run any distinction between areas. However, the same is not true if unemployment exists, or if migration responds imperfectly to labor market inequalities. Areas where unemployment is high can maintain a stable labor force only if remuneration is also high relative to that obtainable elsewhere. Once housing effects are introduced, the picture becomes still more complex; areas in which housing is expensive must also be high-wage areas if they are to prevent net out-migration of labor, other things (such as unemployment rates) being equal. Thus distinct local labor markets can be defined (Topel 1986), in much the same way as distinct local policy jurisdictions within a Tiebout (1956) model; individual preferences determine whether a worker will choose to reside in an area with high rate of joblessness (where wages compensate for the risk of unemployment) or a locality where unemployment is relatively uncommon. Consequently, despite the existence of national (and indeed international) markets for the labor of a minority of very highly skilled workers, the state or metropolitan area makes a more appropriate level for labor market analysis than does the nation.

The second important reason for spatial disaggregation is that it enables us to proceed to an analysis of the reasons why wage rigidity varies across states. This is the main contribution of chapter 3. The analysis builds upon the contribution of Grubb, Jackman and Layard (1983), but by studying regions within a single country (rather than a cross section of OECD nations) we are able to provide a reasonably homogeneous social, cultural, political, and institutional setting.

A third reason for conducting our analyses at the state and local level is that it allows us to study regional variations in labor market behavior across the country. A number of hypotheses can thus be tested. For example: do labor markets in some states (such as those in the Rust-Belt which have endured rapid structural decline) respond differently to economic shocks than do other states? If so, would different labor market policies be appropriate in different regions? Is wage inflation transmitted across the country according to an established set of geographical patterns (Martin 1981)?

To summarize briefly: we estimate separately for 48 states and 16 metropolitan areas the parameters of our labor market model. This enables us to draw important and novel inferences about the dynamics of unemployment, and regional differences in the operation of the labor market can be identified. Since the flexibility of wages varies substantially across the states, we are also able to analyze the determinants of real wage induration. These contributions all have important policy implications: they tell us what counter-unemployment policies might be effective in the various regions of the country, and they suggest measures that could be taken to make wages more responsive to the swings of the market.

Structure of This Book

In chapter 2 we develop the theory and conduct the empirical time series analyses. The theoretical and empirical models build on previous work and involve the simultaneous estimation of Phillips and Fisher curve equations. Variants of our model are tested and a preferred set of results is identified. Thus we can comment upon regional patterns emerging from the results and identify areas within which demand- or supply-side policies would be appropriate as means of alleviating the problem of unemployment. Both states and metropolitan areas are used as bases for our analysis in this chapter; metropolitan areas are particularly interesting because they most nearly approximate the size of local labor market within which we believe most employment decisions are made. The novelty of chapter 2 is primarily seen in the extent of disaggregation used: for the first time, Phillips and Fisher curve estimates are presented for all 48 contiguous states and for 16 cities.

The slopes of the Phillips curves estimated in chapter 2 are a vital input into the work reported in the following chapter. The work reported in chapter 3, using these coefficients, represents what we believe to be the most important original contribution of this book. There we provide an empirical investigation of the differences in measured wage flexibility between the 48 contiguous states. As we have already seen, the received literature is strong on theory concerning wage inflexibilities, but only a handful of rather speculative papers have treated this important issue from an empirical standpoint. By conducting a cross-section analysis of 48 states, we gain significant new insights. We investigate the role of efficiency wages, insider-outsider effects, union behavior, welfare benefits, industrial concentration, and other factors on the flexibility of wages. The results are interesting and policy-relevant.

The final chapter of the book draws together the main results and conclusions. It also contains an extended discussion of the policy implication of our findings.

2

Regional Wage Inflation and Unemployment

This chapter examines the cyclical interaction of wage inflation and unemployment in order to determine the extent to which wage flexibility varies across regional labor markets in the United States. We follow Coe (1985) and Grubb, Jackman and Layard (1983) in measuring wage flexibility as the coefficient on the unemployment rate in a Phillips-type wage adjustment equation. Thus we define regional labor markets with highly flexible wages as those with a relatively large estimated responsiveness of money wage inflation to the unemployment rate.

The Phillips (1958) model of the wage adjustment process is built on the hypothesis that a greater degree of labor market slack, as measured by the unemployment rate, causes a slower rate of wage inflation, other things equal. However, it is clearly possible for causation to run from wage inflation to unemployment. *Ceteris paribus*, a rise in the rate of money wage inflation could be expected to result in a rise in the unemployment rate if wages were rising faster than the marginal revenue product. In order to adjust for the simultaneous relationship between wage inflation and unemployment that could bias the coefficient estimates we use to measure wage flexibility, we specify and estimate a two-equation labor market model that treats wage inflation and unemployment as jointly endogenous variables.

Our primary test for regional differences in wage flexibility focuses on estimates of our regional labor market model on annual data covering the period from 1964 to 1986 for each of the 48 contiguous states. Some might argue that the state is too large an area to be observationally equivalent to a regional labor market. However, data limitations and changes in area definitions limit the number of metropolitan areas for which adequate time series can be constructed. We do present estimates

17

for 16 large metropolitan areas as a check on the results from state data. Anticipating the conclusions from this part of the study, we find that the model fits the time series pattern of unemployment and wage inflation rates for almost all of the states and metropolitan areas studied and that there is evidence of substantial regional variation in the responsiveness of wage inflation to unemployment.

Regional Labor Market Model

Our time series model of the rates of wage inflation and unemployment is very similar to the "simple two-equation structural model of the economy" used by Hall (1975, p. 303) and the three-equation model employed by Layard and Bean (1989). In both of these papers, wage inflation is determined by the unemployment rate and expected price inflation; with cost-plus pricing, unemployment is determined by the interaction of money supply growth and wage inflation. While Hall as well as Layard and Bean use their models to study the characteristics of long-run, equilibrium unemployment rates, our interest is in developing this approach as a means of estimating short-run cyclical movements in wage inflation and unemployment.

Expanding Hall's unemployment equation to take into account unemployment persistence and a broader measure of aggregate demand growth, we specify the following model:

$$w_t = \alpha_0 + \alpha_1 U_t + \alpha_2 p_{t-1} + \epsilon_1 \tag{2.1}$$

$$U_t = \beta_0 + \beta_1 U_{t-1} + \beta_2 y_t + \beta_3 w_t + \epsilon_2 \tag{2.2}$$

Where w is money wage inflation, U is the unemployment rate, p is the rate of change of consumer prices, y is the percentage change of nominal gross product in the regional economy, and ϵ_1 and ϵ_2 are random error terms.

Equation (2.1) presents the wage adjustment process in terms of a conventional Phillips curve relationship. Excess supply in the labor market dampens wage inflation by lowering the reservation wage of unemployed outsiders and by reducing the bargaining strength of insiders. Expected price inflation, measured in equation (2.1) as a function of lagged price inflation, also feeds through into the determination of the rate of change of money wages, since workers base their labor supply decisions on (their perceptions of) the real wage. Our choice of a parsimonious Phillips curve specification is influenced by the careful investigation of alternative Phillips curve specifications by Coe (1985) and by the results of our previous studies (Hyclak and Johnes 1989 and 1992; Johnes and Hyclak 1989). The estimates of the coefficient α_1 serve as our index of regional wage flexibility.

The unemployment rate model in equation (2.2) is not standard in the literature, although Clark (1981) estimates a quite similar equation for Canadian provinces. Thus this relationship requires a more detailed discussion than does the Phillips curve. We refer to this relationship as a Fisher curve after Irving Fisher's (1926) analysis of regressions showing a strong positive relationship between a distributed lag on product prices and the level of employment. Fisher's explanation for this empirical result focused on the effects of demand increases relative to wage levels. He argued that wages and other input costs were relatively fixed in the short run and that an increase in demand which raised selling prices in the short run would result in an increase in labor demand. We call equation (2.2) a Fisher curve because it embodies a similar explanation for unemployment. Unemployment in that equation depends on the growth of demand, measured by the rate of change of nominal Gross State Product (y_t), relative to the rate of change in money wages.

The main determinant of unemployment in this model is the rate of change of aggregate demand for goods produced in the regional labor market. This demand emphasis is consistent with the stylized facts about the cyclical behavior of U.S. labor markets and the evidence on the role of demand shocks in determining changes in local employment discussed in the preceding chapter. We assume that y_t is exogenous because this variable can be treated as being determined largely by national monetary policy and by export demand (Beare 1976). The split of demand growth into real output changes and price changes is endogenous and in large part depends on the responsiveness of wage inflation to changes in unemployment. In the appendix to this study we check the sensitivity of our estimates to this assumption that local demand growth is exogenous.

The current unemployment rate is also expected to be positively related to lagged unemployment. As discussed in chapter 1, Barro (1988), among others, presents evidence of a substantial degree of unemployment persistence for all western economies. One possible explanation for this empirical regularity is that high unemployment in the past leads to a large number of long-term unemployed in the current period. The long-term unemployed may be increasingly ineffective in finding employment due to low morale, skill deterioration, and/or employer screening (Blanchard and Summers 1987).

Equation (2.2) can be derived from two simple but often-used relationships in macroeconomics. The first is normal cost mark-up pricing, as expressed in equation (2.3) below.

The rate of product price inflation equals the rate of wage inflation adjusted for the potential rate of productivity growth,

$$d_t = w_t - (q_t^* - N_t^*). \tag{2.3}$$

Here d_t is producer price inflation, q_t^* is the rate of real potential output growth, and N_t^* is the rate of potential employment growth.

The second relationship is a dynamic version of Okun's law relating changes in the unemployment rate to the net effect of nominal demand growth, potential output growth and price inflation. This can be written as :

$$U_t = U_{t-1} + \Theta(y_t - q_t^* - d_t). \tag{2.4}$$

Substituting equation (2.3) into equation (2.4) yields a relationship like our Fisher curve with clear hypotheses about the coefficients in the relationship. The coefficient on U_{t-1} is hypothesized to equal 1.0, and those on y_t and w_t are hypothesized to be equal in magnitude but with opposite signs. Interestingly, estimates for the United States as a whole for the postwar period cannot reject these hypotheses about the coefficients of the Fisher curve (Hyclak and Johnes 1990).

Of course, these parameter hypotheses depend on the underlying simple model. If, for example, the mark-up rate depends on current economic activity, and lagged unemployment and wage inflation influence current unemployment by labor supply as well as demand effects, the parameter hypotheses of the resulting Fisher curve could be quite different. Nevertheless, this exercise gives us some insight into the derivation of our Fisher curve and leads us to expect values of β_1 in equation (2.2) that lie close to 1.0 and estimates of β_2 and β_3 that are similar in magnitude but of opposite signs.

Although our two-equation labor market model is far too simple to be considered a complete econometric model of regional labor markets, it does offer a number of advantages for the purpose of estimating regional differences in wage flexibility. First, it gives us a way of treating nominal wage inflation and the unemployment rate as jointly endogenous variables, thereby addressing the potentially serious problem of simultaneity bias in our estimates of the wage flexibility coefficients. Second, the model incorporates the concepts of wage rigidity and persistence in explaining the effects of demand shocks on unemployment. A sustained drop in demand growth causes a sustained rise in unemployment unless wage inflation falls far enough and fast enough to offset the effect of the demand slowdown. We use this feature of the model to conduct simulations of the effects of changes in demand growth on unemployment under various wage flexibility conditions. Finally, the model can be estimated with available time series data for the states and some metropolitan areas. This is a considerable advantage, since data availability is perhaps the most significant constraint on regional economic research.

The basic weakness of this model is that it does not directly consider supply-side effects, such as migration and changes in labor force participation, on the local unemployment rate. These forces are captured, if at all, by the intercept of the Fisher curve. However, given the conclusions of Topel (1986), Holzer (1991) and Bartik (1991), discussed in chapter 1, our emphasis on demand-related determinants of unemployment might not be misplaced. And, after all, our primary purpose in estimating the model is to determine the extent to which wage flexibility varies across regional labor markets rather than to model all possible determinants of unemployment.

Empirical Analysis

In previous studies we have used the model described above to study regional wage and unemployment dynamics in Great Britain (Hyclak and Johnes 1992), and to produce an international comparison over a long period of cyclical movements in the labor market (Hyclak and Johnes 1990). The analyses in this section use data for the years 1964 through 1986, collected for the 48 contiguous states and 16 large metropolitan areas of the United States.

The main software package used to perform the statistical analyses is RATS, version 3.01. Data have been analysed using the three-stage least squares (3SLS) method. A separate two-equation system, based upon the theoretical model of equations (2.1) and (2.2), has thus been estimated for each state. The Appendix presents a comparison of the 3SLS results reported here with those obtained by ordinary least squares (OLS) and two-stage least squares (2SLS). That comparison suggests that for most states the method of estimation makes no significant difference in the parameter estimates. This is especially the case for the wage flexibility coefficients, for which the OLS, 2SLS, and 3SLS estimates are all highly correlated across the states. For some states, however, Hausman tests indicate that 3SLS is the appropriate estimator; we present just those results here to make cross-state comparisons easier and more consistent.

Wage inflation is measured as the rate of change in average hourly earnings in manufacturing using data obtained from various issues of the *Handbook of Labor Statistics*. Two types of compositional effects in the cyclical movement of this variable need to be recognized, even though there is little we can do to correct for them. During a recession, less senior, lower-wage employees are likely to be laid off first, in which case the use of average earnings might overstate the true rate of change in wages. Working to understate the true rate of change when average earnings are used to measure wage inflation is the fact that layoffs are more prominent in the higher paying durable goods manufacturing industries. In any case, average hourly earnings in manufacturing is the only wage measure for which we can obtain a sufficiently long time series for all states.

The unemployment rate data for each state are taken from two sources. Data for the earlier years in our sample are estimates based on unemployment insurance and other workforce records, the so-called "handbook method," and taken from various issues of the *Manpower Report of the President*. Data for later years are unemployment estimates derived from the Current Population Survey and supplied by the Bureau of Labor Statistics. For the 10 largest states, the survey data were first available in 1967. Current Population Survey unemployment rates are available for 16 additional states beginning in 1970, for 2 states starting in 1972, and for the remaining states in 1976. Inspection of the data for overlapping years indicated that the handbook estimates generally fell within the error range at a 90 percent confidence level of the survey estimates.

Consumer price inflation is measured as the rate of change in the personal consumption expenditures deflator using data from the *Economic Report of the President*. No local price data exist for states, hence the use of a national measure of consumer price inflation. The results reported below for metropolitan areas do use local consumer price index data in some of the estimates. Finally, the rate of change in aggregate spending on goods and services produced in the region is measured by the percent change in nominal Gross State Product (GSP). Annual GSP estimates for 1963–1986 were kindly provided by the U.S. Department of Commerce.

The choice of instrumental variables can obviously be a matter of considerable importance when estimating the parameters of a system of equations. The specification of the equations being estimated should, of course, be chosen so as to ensure that the coefficients are reasonably robust with respect to the choice of instruments; our early experiments confirmed that this is the case with our chosen model. That condition being satisfied, our choice of instruments has been governed by the requirement that the model should provide good forecasts of the endogenous variables (both within and outside the sample period), while ensuring also that the specification remains parsimonious. To this end, our experimentation with various sets of instruments has been extensive. Our preferred set of instruments consists of the exogenous variables which appear in the two-equation system, plus the lagged national percentage growth rates of real Gross National Product (GNP) and hourly earnings in manufacturing.

The estimated Phillips curves for each state are reported in table 2.1. A glance at the coefficients indicates that there are few surprises. In all the states bar two (Connecticut and New Mexico), unemployment affects wage inflation in the expected negative direction. In the two atypical cases, the coefficient on unemployment does not differ significantly from zero. Unemployment exerts a significantly negative impact on wages (at the 5 percent level) in 32 of the 48 states.

The results for Connecticut and New Mexico suggest the presence of complete hysteresis in wage adjustment in those labor markets. Hysteresis has received considerable attention in recent attempts to explain unemployment persistence (see, for example, Blanchard and Summers 1987; Johnson and Layard 1986; and Lindbeck and Snower 1988). One implication of the hysteresis process is that wages may be responsive only to changes in unemployment and completely unresponsive to the level of unemployment, regardless of how high unemployment rates become.

In order to test this implication of hysteresis for the wage adjustment process, we employed a Phillips curve specification developed by Franz (1987). By including the current and lagged unemployment rates in the equation, it is possible to interpret the sum of the coefficients on these two variables as the effect of the level of unemployment on wage inflation and the negative of the coefficient on lagged unemployment as the effect of changes in unemployment on wage inflation. Results of these estimates, not reported here but available from the authors, indicate that the level effect for both Connecticut and New Mexico is not significantly different from zero, but that changes in unemployment have a statistically significant impact on wage inflation at the 5 percent level for Connecticut and the 10 percent level for New Mexico.

Partial hysteresis effects, where both the level of and change in

Table 2.1   Phillips Curve Estimates, 48 States, 1964–1986

$$w_t^i = \alpha_0 + \alpha_1 U_t^i + \alpha p_{t-1}^{US}$$

	α_0	α_1	α_2	R^2	d	RESET	Jarque-Bera
New England:							
ME	3.96	−.3731	.9745	.7781	1.362	1.6750	.5847
	(1.12)	(.2519)	(.1496)				
NH	4.59	−.3813	.7241	.7158	1.722	2.4870	.5382
	(.54)	(.1863)	(.1169)				
VT	6.23	−.7277	.8565	.7605	1.569	.1183	1.4795
	(.88)	(.2000)	(.1036)				
MA	3.96	−.1199	.5633	.6588	1.412	2.7040	4.1782
	(.59)	(.1343)	(.0961)				
RI	4.29	−.3698	.7643	.6459	2.076	.2730	2.3461
	(.69)	(.1927)	(.1315)				
CT	2.59	.0987	.5678	.6929	1.977	2.0542	1.9318
	(.74)	(.1629)	(.1059)				
Middle Atlantic:							
NY	3.17	−.0907	.6697	.7014	1.192	2.4778	.4659
	(.77)	(.1668)	(.1213)				
NJ	2.61	−.0788	.7530	.6932	1.308	.4940	1.5194
	(.91)	(.2058)	(.1477)				
PA	5.19	−.6699	.9991	.6789	1.299	.5062	.4414
	(.98)	(.1799)	(.1511)				
East North Central:							
OH	4.01	−.5334	1.0982	.6821	2.328	.4526	1.9047
	(.89)	(.1587)	(.1583)				
IN	4.70	−.9089	1.3303	.7760	2.004	.6587	.6525
	(.79)	(.1739)	(.1698)				
IL	4.38	−.5893	1.011	.7765	2.048	.1899	.5246
	(.71)	(.1269)	(.1210)				
MI	4.61	−.5402	1.1846	.6385	2.155	.1901	2.1031
	(1.08)	(.1934)	(.2413)				
WI	4.95	−.8615	1.1227	.8882	1.915	2.4450	1.4324
	(.57)	(.1185)	(.0942)				
West North Central:							
MN	4.64	−.7902	1.016	.7853	2.159	2.0230	.4685
	(.99)	(.2357)	(.1140)				
IA	4.71	−1.1596	1.2382	.7761	1.655	1.7310	1.4799
	(.92)	(.1877)	(.1449)				

Table 2.1   (*continued*)

	α_0	α_1	α_2	R^2	d	RESET	Jarque-Bera
MO	4.55	−.5922	.9066	.7265	1.829	.8122	11.5260
	(.81)	(.1874)	(.1317)				
ND	14.32	−2.9014	.8641	.7253	2.244	.5808	.7133
	(3.87)	(.7819)	(.1843)				
SD	9.11	−2.5447	1.1603	.6827	1.536	.1011	.6459
	(2.70)	(.7455)	(.2210)				
NE	6.00	−1.5057	1.0650	.6825	2.265	.4785	1.1338
	(1.32)	(.3808)	(.1455)				
KS	4.46	−1.0148	1.0817	.6287	1.661	.5994	1.4652
	(2.19)	(.5543)	(.1921)				
South Atlantic:							
DE	3.11	−.0611	.6432	.2735	2.171	.4329	.1263
	(1.59)	(.4643)	(.3165)				
MD	6.30	−1.4564	1.3808	.5743	1.790	.6593	1.3408
	(1.46)	(.4697)	(.2568)				
VA	5.03	−.8015	1.0150	.7245	1.690	.4056	2.1109
	(1.04)	(.3483)	(.1661)				
WV	5.61	−.5266	.9850	.8001	1.583	1.3370	1.6052
	(1.04)	(.1022)	(.1193)				
NC	7.12	−.9691	.8995	.7215	2.178	1.2780	2.4433
	(.93)	(.2366)	(.1386)				
SC	6.87	−.8213	.9557	.7340	1.790	.3307	1.1888
	(1.05)	(.2263)	(.1479)				
GA	5.63	−.4769	.7080	.5806	1.562	.0646	.2577
	(.94)	(.2470)	(.1423)				
FL	5.16	−.9146	1.1770	.7140	1.151	3.5950	1.5844
	(1.01)	(.2780)	(.1963)				
East South Central:							
KY	5.80	−.5733	.8059	.6424	1.739	.7688	.5271
	(.92)	(.1445)	(.1207)				
TN	4.80	−.4719	.8918	.6722	1.838	.4582	2.3728
	(.82)	(.1536)	(.1354)				
AL	4.66	−.4251	.8888	.6132	1.465	.5505	2.0639
	(.88)	(.1299)	(.1345)				
MS	5.62	−.3694	.6778	.4415	2.542	.5506	.1251
	(1.34)	(.1837)	(.1693)				
West South Central:							
AR	7.12	−.9556	1.1188	.7479	2.366	.1880	.2667
	(1.23)	(.2260)	(.1602)				

Table 2.1 (*continued*)

	α_0	α_1	α_2	R^2	d	RESET	Jarque-Bera
LA	5.01	-.5174	1.0475	.7575	2.276	.8400	.0442
	(1.19)	(.1497)	(.1251)				
OK	5.39	-.9339	1.0856	.8243	1.889	.4461	.6063
	(1.28)	(.2286)	(.1366)				
TX	5.71	-1.0152	1.0926	.8958	1.896	.2433	.5421
	(1.09)	(.2101)	(.1072)				
Mountain:							
MT	8.77	-1.1704	.9236	.2191	1.491	5.0460	7.0058
	(4.20)	(.7187)	(.2815)				
ID	7.42	-.8741	.7918	.3182	2.477	.7534	1.007
	(2.05)	(.3799)	(.2196)				
WY	5.21	-.7400	.7627	.2981	2.496	.0924	3.9364
	(3.16)	(.5473)	(.2697)				
CO	4.60	-.8491	1.0054	.5991	1.586	.4937	1.1313
	(1.36)	(.3641)	(.1802)				
NM	-.78	.1212	1.1297	.7127	2.558	.7827	.6952
	(2.24)	(.3813)	(.1974)				
AZ	2.98	-.6924	1.3360	.7604	1.838	1.1510	1.6839
	(1.24)	(.2866)	(.2179)				
UT	8.40	-1.4578	1.1259	.7120	1.753	.5683	.5063
	(2.19)	(.4015)	(.1477)				
NV	5.08	-.7139	.8769	.4397	1.421	.09289	3.1536
	(1.98)	(.3390)	(.1904)				
Pacific:							
WA	7.36	-1.0962	1.4342	.8233	.805	.1688	1.2048
	(1.48)	(.2247)	(.1645)				
OR	6.93	-1.2040	1.4831	.8068	1.508	1.6280	1.6467
	(1.04)	(.1995)	(.1619)				
CA	5.74	-.8158	1.1115	.9030	1.369	.2920	.7514
	(1.08)	(.1839)	(.0929)				

Estimated using 3 stage least squares. Standard errors in parentheses. R^2 is from a regression of actual wage inflation on that forecast by the model.

Figure 2.1 Geographical Pattern of Wage Flexibility Coefficients

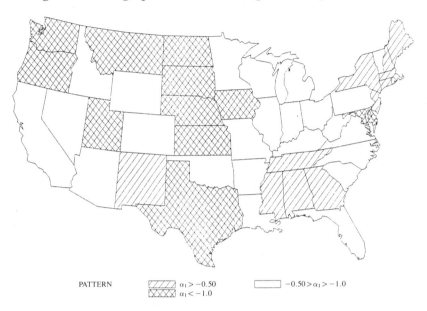

PATTERN $\alpha_1 > -0.50$ $-0.50 > \alpha_1 > -1.0$
             $\alpha_1 < -1.0$

unemployment are significant determinants of wage inflation, were found for the older industrial states of Pennsylvania, Ohio, Michigan, Indiana, and Missouri, as well as for Georgia, Idaho, and Oregon. Since the change in unemployment was not a statistically significant determinant of wage inflation for most states and since the level effect of unemployment in these regressions is highly correlated with the estimates of α_1 reported in table 2.1, we concentrate our attention on the results obtained from the simple Phillips curve specification developed in the section above.

As can be seen from the map shown in figure 2.1, the unemployment coefficients reported in table 2.1 exhibit a pronounced spatial pattern. They tend to be close to zero in the Northeast and, interestingly, in the South Central states, but often exceed unity (in absolute terms) in the Pacific and West North Central states. These findings are very much in accord with those of Blackley (1989). Chi-square tests reject the null hypothesis that $\alpha_1 = -.78$, the mean value of α_1 across the 48 states, for

15 states at the five percent level and for an additional 4 states at the ten percent level. These results suggest there was considerable variation in wage flexibility across the 48 states during the 1964–1986 sample period.

Theory predicts that the coefficient on the expected price inflation term in the Phillips curve should lie close to unity. Despite our choice of an extremely simple form of expectations formation, this prediction is fulfilled in all but a very few states. In all states, this coefficient significantly exceeds zero at the 5 percent level. Only for New Hampshire, Massachussetts, Connecticut, Georgia, and Mississippi is this coefficient significantly below one at the same level; for Oregon and Washington the coefficient significantly exceeds one.

The coefficients of determination are reported in table 2.1 alongside the regression equations. The R^2 statistics here are those of an OLS regression of actual wage inflation on that forecast in a static fashion by the model. The fit of the estimated Phillips curve to the data is sound in almost every case. Four of the equations do, in this respect, give some cause for concern, however. Delaware produces an equation with rather low explanatory power, as do three of the Mountain region states, namely, Montana, Idaho, and Wyoming. The predominance of agriculture and mining in the Mountain region may account in part for the poor performance of the Phillips curve regressions in these states, since the use of manufacturing wages to capture general wage inflation may be inappropriate here. As we shall see later, however, the equation estimated for Montana is unsatisfactory also in certain other respects, and is likely to need further investigation. Delaware is somewhat different; this is an example of a small state whose labor market may be dominated by employment opportunities in neighboring states, so that unemployment conditions within Delaware alone cannot adequately explain real wage movements within the state. These problems will be pursued further in the Appendix.

It is important before proceeding further to test for any violations of the assumptions underlying the 3SLS method used above. The first violation for which we test is that of serial correlation of the regression residuals. The Durbin-Watson statistic, d, is reported for each of the estimated Phillips curves in table 2.1. In one state – Washington – d falls below the lower critical value at both the 5 percent and 1 percent levels of significance. The remaining states all have Durbin-Watson statistics acceptably close to the ideal value.

We next conduct a test for misspecification of the Phillips curve equation. The RESET statistic devised by Ramsey (1969) is appropriate here, and should be especially useful as a means of ascertaining whether or not nonlinear terms need to be introduced into the Phillips function. The 5 percent critical value of the second order RESET statistic, as reported in table 2.1, is $F(2,20) = 3.49$. The corresponding 1 percent critical value is 5.85. Of the 48 state-specific Phillips curves, only for Florida and Montana is there significant evidence of misspecification at the 5 percent level. At the 1 percent level, all equations pass the RESET.

Finally, we test for the possibility that the regression residuals are distributed in non-Gaussian fashion. The normality test devised by Jarque and Bera (1980) to check for skewness and kurtosis in the error vector is used here. The Jarque-Bera test statistic follows a chi-square distribution; in the case of the regressions reported in table 2.1, the critical value is 5.99 at the 5 percent significance level. Only two states – Missouri and Montana – fail this test. At the 1 percent significance level, the critical chi-square value is 10.60. Only in Missouri is the non-normality test failed at this level. The presence of non-normally distributed residuals often results from an outlying value of the dependent variable during a single time period. We again investigate this later in the Appendix.

Despite the problems referred to above, the overall performance of this specification of the Phillips curve is good. The estimated equation fits the data closely for all but a few states, yielding sensible coefficients and churning out remarkably few statistical problems.

The 3SLS estimates of the Fisher curve are reported in table 2.2. In general the parameter estimates appear quite plausible for most states, given the hypotheses derived from our simple theory combining Okun's law and cost-plus pricing to yield the Fisher curve. Recall that the theory hypothesizes that β_1, the coefficient on lagged unemployment, equals one and that β_2 and β_3, the coefficients on aggregate demand

Table 2.2 Fisher Curve Estimates, 48 States, 1964–1986

$$U_t^i = \beta_0 + \beta_1 U_{t-1}^i + \beta_2 y_t^i + \beta_3 w_t^i$$

	β_0	β_1	β_2	β_3	R²	d	RESET	Jarque-Bera	h
New England:									
ME	1.29	.8284	−.3079	.3794	.7687	1.858	.1869	1.1607	.6681
	(.91)	(.1794)	(.1132)	(.1033)					
NH	.23	.9371	−.3692	.5894	.8933	2.527	1.2310	1.4919	−1.5080
	(.89)	(.1137)	(.06222)	(.1084)					
VT	1.29	.8520	−.2643	.3051	.8055	2.230	.0700	2.2409	−.6700
	(.90)	(.1184)	(.06227)	(.0958)					
MA	1.53	.8233	−.4048	.4688	.8621	2.324	.1043	1.6085	−.9198
	(1.06)	(.1116)	(.09115)	(.1516)					
RI	.87	.7489	−.3708	.5940	.7877	2.607	1.1310	1.4380	−2.5620
	(1.32)	(.1716)	(.1168)	(.1892)					
CT	2.19	.8116	−.3479	.3121	.8479	1.879	.1792	.8400	.3622
	(.75)	(.1248)	(.0725)	(.1282)					
Middle Atlantic:									
NY	.67	.7746	−.2276	.4208	.8925	1.195	.2399	1.5290	2.1720
	(.90)	(.0956)	(.0913)	(.1045)					
NJ	1.84	.8729	−.4284	.4284	.9120	1.535	.3044	.9756	1.2480
	(.71)	(.0935)	(.0912)	(.0794)					
PA	.77	.9916	−.4735	.4602	.9484	2.039	2.9624	1.4515	−.0999
	(.75)	(.0730)	(.0873)	(.0818)					

Table 2.2 (*continued*)

	β_0	β_1	β_2	β_3	R^2	d	RESET	Jarque-Bera	h
East North Central:									
OH	1.09	.9232	−.3925	.3904	.9683	2.589	1.1602	.34326	−1.4700
	(.55)	(.0577)	(.0475)	(.06628)					
IN	.87	.9064	−.3083	.3393	.9377	3.003	.3304	.1123	−2.514
	(.61)	(.0606)	(.0446)	(.0682)					
IL	.89	.9723	−.3617	.3484	.9565	2.478	.6584	1.0623	−1.187
	(.64)	(.0537)	(.0544)	(.0622)					
MI	.79	.9145	−.3491	.3943	.9220	2.748	.02170	2.5853	−1.866
	(.65)	(.0574)	(.0400)	(.0816)					
WI	.86	.9577	−.3680	.4000	.9278	2.143	.1778	1.4826	−.364
	(.67)	(.0701)	(.0566)	(.0685)					
West North Central:									
MN	.29	.8677	−.1289	.2449	.8016	2.722	1.065	.4212	−2.072
	(.88)	(.1146)	(.0456)	(.0680)					
IA	−.57	1.0386	−.1019	.2206	.9516	2.614	.6225	1.3360	−1.582
	(.59)	(.0763)	(.0243)	(.0515)					
MO	.34	.9548	−.2657	.3468	.8874	2.540	.6661	.9339	−1.404
	(.65)	(.0806)	(.0573)	(.0790)					
ND	−.06	1.0050	−.0305	.0686	.6286	2.0	.1046	1.5984	—
	(1.31)	(.2374)	(.0110)	(.0572)					
SD	−.65	1.0830	−.0302	.1115	.7896	2.350	.2934	1.4812	−1.115
	(.69)	(.1372)	(.0131)	(.0332)					

NB	.14 (.89)	.9223 (.1597)	−.1125 (.0319)	.1828 (.0593)	.8009	2.193	.4923	2.4277	−.719
KS	1.40 (.63)	.8035 (.1245)	−.2070 (.0442)	.2059 (.0545)	.7332	2.289	.3369	.6972	−.863
South Atlantic:									
DE	−.90 (.88)	.5850 (.1231)	−.0647 (.0413)	.6329 (.1365)	.9140	2.350	3.6000	.8470	−1.040
MD	1.09 (.65)	.8550 (.0751)	−.2216 (.0620)	.2708 (.0497)	.9572	1.934	.3068	.2201	.169
VA	.94 (.67)	.7854 (.0908)	−.1897 (.0656)	.2995 (.0618)	.8949	1.743	.3633	.5641	.684
WV	.68 (1.50)	.9161 (.1035)	−.4387 (.1282)	.5433 (.1436)	.8975	1.495	.9016	.5407	1.395
NC	1.50 (.98)	.9889 (.1251)	−.4804 (.0885)	.4654 (.1197)	.8232	2.499	1.0701	.5636	−1.496
SC	1.69 (.79)	.8263 (.0766)	−.3304 (.0505)	.3869 (.0765)	.8782	1.450	1.4650	.9246	1.418
GA	1.30 (.69)	.9435 (.0934)	−.2813 (.0540)	.2945 (.0883)	.8887	1.667	.5690	.4254	.893
FL	2.20 (.94)	.7345 (.0922)	−.2840 (.0639)	.4333 (.0956)	.8684	2.288	.1809	2.4544	−.770
East South Central:									
KY	.49 (.99)	.9441 (.0894)	−.3571 (.0751)	.4611 (.1235)	.9261	2.131	2.6290	1.2101	−.347
TN	.66 (.81)	.9058 (.0705)	−.3130 (.0561)	.4514 (.0896)	.9304	2.080	2.8790	1.7881	−.203

Table 2.2 (continued)

	β_0	β_1	β_2	β_3	R^2	d	RESET	Jarque-Bera	h
AL	.14	.9749	-.3537	.5477	.9400	1.561	.8680	.3056	1.158
	(1.02)	(.0867)	(.0859)	(.1261)					
MS	-1.60	1.0441	-.2708	.6028	.9237	2.184	1.2170	1.9473	-.5031
	(1.22)	(.1002)	(.0548)	(.1521)					
West South Central:									
AR	-.23	.9478	-.1620	.3303	.8523	2.036	.0513	.3450	-.0973
	(.99)	(.0960)	(.0468)	(.0800)					
LA	.52	.9161	-.1452	.2604	.9232	2.102	1.4520	1.0376	-.2705
	(.81)	(.0890)	(.0359)	(.07877)					
OK	2.77	.4756	-.4533	.6292	.9121	1.829	1.5380	.7757	.4521
	(.61)	(.0878)	(.0626)	(.1146)					
TX	1.14	.8755	-.2746	.4005	.8762	2.436	.0492	1.3660	-1.1420
	(.55)	(.0838)	(.0345)	(.0576)					
Mountain:									
MT	.73	.8649	-.1008	.1634	.8252	1.293	1.1480	.9746	2.1550
	(.91)	(.1287)	(.0358)	(.0682)					
ID	-.53	.9579	-.1259	.3242	.8452	2.664	5.2080	.8181	-2.4900
	(1.26)	(.1603)	(.0741)	(.1786)					
WY	.39	.7369	-.1206	.3702	.7915	2.568	6.3350	.0428	—
	(1.44)	(.2362)	(.0590)	(.2242)					
CO	.78	.7735	-.1682	.3729	.7557	2.607	1.6530	.9152	-2.8560
	(1.12)	(.1794)	(.1126)	(.1838)					

NM	2.48	.5624	−.1095	.2942	.7344	1.838	.5022	2.1979	.5650
	(.96)	(.1514)	(.0486)	(.1038)					
AZ	3.28	.6668	−.2716	.3381	.7894	2.003	.7385	.9849	−.0080
	(.84)	(.0932)	(.0482)	(.0788)					
UT	1.94	.7194	−.1225	.1513	.6429	1.709	.0443	.8404	1.1220
	(1.07)	(.1633)	(.0540)	(.0795)					
NV	2.12	.7491	−.2538	.5064	.8428	1.457	4.758	2.5787	2.2670
	(1.34)	(.1707)	(.0750)	(.2053)					
Pacific:									
WA	1.50	.9298	−.2847	.2781	.8742	2.593	.3021	1.5591	−1.5630
	(.82)	(.0866)	(.0476)	(.0594)					
OR	1.00	.8992	−.2064	.2769	.9410	1.236	.2833	1.0762	1.9260
	(.63)	(.0643)	(.0359)	(.0548)					
CA	1.90	1.0190	−.4122	.3356	.8398	2.180	.1687	6.5694	−.5147
	(.75)	(.1136)	(.0734)	(.0625)					

Estimated using three stage least squares. Standard errors in parentheses. R^2 from a regression of actual unemployment on that forecast by the model.

growth and wage inflation, should sum to zero. These hypotheses about the Fisher curve parameters cannot be rejected for the vast majority of states in our sample.

Chi-square tests reject the null hypothesis that $\beta_1 = 1$ at the 5 percent level for just nine states: New York, Delaware, Maryland, Virginia, South Carolina, Florida, Oklahoma, New Mexico, and Arizona. Since a number of these states have experienced significant net migration during the sample period (see Smith and Ahmed 1990), perhaps a coefficient on U_{t-1} that is significantly below unity reflects the impact of lagged unemployment on labor supply in the current period. If high unemployment reduced net in-migration or speeded up net out-migration, we might expect a subsequent drop in unemployment even if demand growth and wage inflation were unchanged.

Chi-square tests reject the null hypothesis that $\beta_2 + \beta_3 = 0$ at the five percent level for nine states. In this case the states are Iowa, South Dakota, Delaware, Mississippi, Arkansas, Louisiana, Oklahoma, Texas, and New Mexico. Interestingly, the last six of these states are all clustered together. Perhaps the Okun's law-cost-plus pricing relationships are inappropriate for these economies with oil, other natural resources, and agriculture as dominant industries. Still, our simple unemployment rate equation emphasizing aggregate demand effects on unemployment seems to fit the data quite well for most of the states.

The closeness of fit achieved by the Fisher curve equations is uniformly good, as evidenced by the high determination coefficient attached to each regression. This is encouraging, since it means that the ability of the model to make accurate within-sample forecasts of unemployment is strong.

In the case of the Fisher curve, the Durbin-Watson d test for residual autocorrelation cannot legitimately be used, since this test is biased when a lagged dependent variable appears on the right-hand side of the estimated equation. We therefore use Durbin's h test in order to identify any violations of the assumption of serial independence in the error vector. The 1 and 5 percent critical values for this test are, respectively, 2.58 and 1.96. The h statistics reported in table 2.2 indicate that serial correlation is not a widespread problem, although the h statistic is significant at the 5 percent level for some eight states. Only in the case of Colorado is the serial correlation significant at 1 percent. We correct for this problem in the Appendix.

The RESET statistics shown in table 2.2 indicate that the Fisher curve is well specified in most cases. In four states, however, the RESET statistic exceeds the 5 percent critical value. In two states — Idaho and Wyoming — the RESET test is failed at 1 percent significance. It is instructive to note that both these states produced low determination coefficients in the Phillips curve estimates. The possibility that these two problems are related will be investigated further at a later stage.

The Jarque-Bera test for off-white noise vectors may now be considered. At the 5 percent level, this indicates that residuals are normally distributed in all states but one — the exception is California. If the test is repeated at 1 percent significance, the null hypothesis of normally distributed residuals is accepted for all 48 states under consideration.

Hitherto, the suite of tests with which we have confronted the model has consisted of tests on single coefficients or single equations. Further statistical problems might conceivably arise, however, as a consequence of interactions between the local economies of the 48 contiguous states. The construction of a test to check for this possibility occupies the remainder of the present section.

A large body of literature has in recent years grown around the possibility that inflationary pressures are transmitted between regions according to a stable and well-defined system of trails. The contributions of Lesage and Reed (1989, 1990), Blackaby and Manning (1990), and Hyclak and Johnes (1992) are relevant in this context. The central ideas are not new, however; papers of an older vintage by Thirlwall (1969, 1970) and Mackay and Hart (1975) concern similar issues.

In the present exercise, any attempt to establish the existence of spatial transmission mechanisms for wage inflation is likely to be rendered difficult by the use of annual (rather than quarterly or monthly) data. Nevertheless it is prudent to conduct a test for such mechanisms. If a test indicates that some states or regions play the role of wage leaders, correct specification of the Phillips curves for the remaining states would require the inclusion of leader-state inflation as an explanatory variable.

Two methods are used in order to test the hypothesis that a spatial wage transmission mechanism operates within the continental United States. The first method involves comparing, on the one hand, the correlation matrix associated with the 48 state-specific residual vectors obtained from the 3SLS Phillips curve regressions, and on the other hand, the 48th order identity matrix. These turn out to be very similar. Ideally we would wish to conduct a chi-square test of homogeneity between these two matrices, but the presence of many zeros in the identity matrix would substantially weaken the power of any such test.

We have also used this method to check for the simultaneous existence of spatial and temporal serial correlation. In the latter case the correlation matrix contains also the state-specific vectors of lagged noise terms, and the corresponding identity matrix is of order 96. Again we found no evidence to support the hypothesis that inflation is transmitted through the states via an established mechanism.

In addition to the above broad brush procedure, extensive tests of the wage transmission hypothesis have been conducted at the level of the individual state. These experiments consisted of the insertion into the Phillips curve of lagged wage inflation in contiguous states. These trials met with limited success; the newly introduced term never turned out to be statistically significant at conventional levels.

In this section the basic set of time series results has been obtained. This includes estimates of the state-specific Phillips and Fisher curves. In most states the model passes through our exacting series of tests with flying colors. For a small minority of states, statistical checks indicate that there may be difficulties caused by outlying or serially correlated error terms, or by specification problems. In the Appendix we have attempted to correct for the statistical problems identified for a handful of states. The results of that exercise leave unchanged our basic results on the spatial variation in the unemployment responsiveness of wage inflation. Additionally, we have examined the sensitivity of our estimates to differences in estimating methods and to the assumption that local demand growth is exogenous. We find with these results, also reported in the Appendix, that our coefficient estimates, particularly those of α_1, are not materially affected by these changes. That said, the coefficient estimates for all states appear sensible in that they accord with theory and the overall performance of the model is very good indeed.

Metropolitan Areas

Hitherto, the analysis has concerned data collected at the level of the state. In this section we investigate the performance of the basic model when applied to data disaggregated to a finer level — that of the metropolitan area. The local labor market is, of course, the arena within which the forces acting upon wages and unemployment operate. Given the relatively small number of long distance commuters, it is wage (and non-price) competition between local employers that determines the allocation of labor (at least in the short run when migration cannot occur). This being so, any satisfactory model of the labor market should work well at the level of the local labor market.

The data requirements of our model can be satisfied over a fairly long time period for most of the large metropolitan areas of the United States. Annual Current Population Survey (CPS) estimates of unemployment rates are available for 20 such areas over the period 1967–1986. Local price indices for the same 20 local labor markets are available throughout this period from the Bureau of Labor Statistics and are published in the *Statistical Abstract*. For all but four of these areas (Los Angeles, San Francisco, Newark, and Paterson), a complete run of wage data is also available. The wage data for the four remaining areas have not been reported since 1980; unfortunately, therefore, the available information provides insufficient degrees of freedom for us to estimate with confidence the parameters of the model in these cases. Consequently, our attention will be focused upon the remaining 16 metropolitan areas.

In the absence of an official time series for the nominal Gross City Product of individual metropolitan areas, we have proxied the rate of growth of this variable by the rate of growth of the relevant Gross State Product. In some cases, metropolitan areas cross state lines. Thus the

Philadelphia area comprises parts of both Pennsylvania and New Jersey; St. Louis straddles the Missouri and Illinois state line; Minneapolis-St. Paul bestrides the boundary between Minnesota and Wisconsin. Other metropolitan areas include portions of three states. Cincinnati lies in the tri-state area which comprises Ohio, Kentucky and Indiana; and the nation's capital includes parts of Maryland and Virginia as well as the whole of the District of Columbia. In all these cases we have proxied the rate of growth of aggregate demand in the metropolitan area by the weighted average rate of aggregate demand growth in all states within which lie parts of the local labor market of interest.

Table 2.3 shows the estimated Phillips curve equations. These follow much the same pattern as do the corresponding equations at the level of the state. Interpreting the coefficient on unemployment as a measure of wage flexibility, metropolitan areas in Maryland and Texas are characterised by relatively flexible wages, while those in the Northeast are comparatively rigid. The coefficient on unemployment carries the expected negative sign in all areas bar one, and is significantly different from zero in most of these areas; the odd area out is Boston, where the coefficient is insignificant. The coefficient on expected price inflation is of reasonable magnitude in all areas, again with the single exception of Boston.

The relatively poor performance of the equation for Boston suggests that there may be a statistical problem here. This is confirmed by the diagnostics; a significantly high RESET value implies the presence of functional misspecification in the Boston area Phillips curve. The only other problems identified by our diagnostics is the non-normal distribution of the residuals in the Dallas-Fort Worth equation, and possibly also in Washington DC. These problems are addressed in the Appendix.

The Fisher curve estimates for metropolitan areas appear in table 2.4. The estimated coefficients generally have plausible magnitudes, and the standard errors are, in general, low in relation to the means. Unemployment persistence is to be observed to a marked degree in almost all areas. Indeed, in 10 of the areas studied, the estimated coefficient on lagged unemployment does not differ significantly from one at the 5 percent level. The parameter estimates generally indicate wage inflation

Table 2.3 Phillips Curve Estimates, 16 Large SMSAs, 1964–86

$$w_t^i = \alpha_0 + \alpha_1 U_t^i + \alpha_2 p_{t-1}^{US}$$

Area	α_0	α_1	α_2	R^2	d	RESET	Jarque-Bera
New York	4.02	−.30	.72	.72	1.95	1.44	1.24
	(.68)	(.14)	(.12)				
Chicago	3.27	−.26	.82	.67	1.72	0.36	1.90
	(.69)	(.12)	(.12)				
Philadelphia	4.50	−.44	.86	.63	1.52	0.27	1.52
	(.95)	(.24)	(.18)				
Detroit	4.82	−.52	1.16	.58	1.86	0.50	1.47
	(1.04)	(.18)	(.24)				
Boston	3.92	.03	.41	.54	1.18	9.36	1.10
	(.61)	(.15)	(.10)				
Washington	8.27	−2.92	1.78	.12	1.38	0.92	7.51
	(4.69)	(2.04)	(.81)				
Pittsburgh	4.03	−.62	1.18	.64	1.86	3.91	3.90
	(1.38)	(.18)	(.19)				
St. Louis	4.02	−.32	.82	.69	1.36	2.57	0.68
	(0.82)	(.17)	(.13)				
Cleveland	4.38	−.58	1.02	.62	2.06	0.30	1.64
	(1.14)	(.21)	(.20)				
Baltimore	6.01	−1.38	1.54	.65	1.47	1.06	0.76
	(1.41)	(.42)	(.29)				
Dallas–Fort Worth	4.98	−.95	1.03	.62	2.20	0.40	13.53
	(1.54)	(.43)	(.17)				
Houston	4.57	−.84	1.14	.82	2.56	0.16	1.24
	(1.22)	(.20)	(.14)				
Milwaukee	4.14	−.69	1.12	.86	2.08	1.89	0.99
	(0.58)	(.11)	(.10)				
Minneapolis– St. Paul	2.82	−.22	.84	.72	1.14	1.15	0.74
	(.94)	(.26)	(.14)				
Cincinnati	2.98	−.30	1.01	.56	1.82	3.65	0.58
	(1.03)	(.18)	(.19)				
Buffalo	2.64	−.06	.80	.42	1.26	1.53	0.40
	(1.44)	(.24)	(.24)				

Standard errors in parentheses. Estimated using three stage least squares. R^2 refers to that generated by a regression of actual on forecast values derived from static, in-sample forecasts of W_t and U_t.

and demand growth coefficients which lie within a plausible range; the only exception is Washington DC, where the coefficient on wage inflation is somewhat lower than expected. The diagnostic tests also highlight Washington as an area where the Fisher curve may run into statistical problems. The RESET statistic is significantly high, thus pointing to possible misspecification of the function. This misspecification may, of course, be related to the presence of outlying residuals observed in this area's Phillips curve. In addition, two areas have Fisher curves plagued by serial correlation of the residuals, as evidenced by Durbin's h statistic. These areas are Detroit and Minneapolis-St. Paul.

In table 2.5 we report estimates of the Phillips curve for the 15 large metropolitan areas in which the lagged rate of consumer price inflation is measured with local Consumer Price Indexes (CPI) rather than the national Personal Consumption Expenditures Deflator (PCED). The effect of this change on the estimated coefficients is quite marked. The estimates of α_1 are generally lower in magnitude and smaller relative to the standard errors in table 2.5 in comparison with the results in table 2.3. Use of the local CPI data also results in lower estimates of the coefficient on lagged price inflation and lower Durbin-Watson statistics, suggesting the presence of serial correlation in the residuals.

Measurement error in the CPI, related to the treatment of mortgage interest rates prior to 1983, has led Gordon (1990b), among others, to conclude that the PCED is a more accurate measure of consumer price inflation than the CPI, particularly for the 1970s. The fact that the PCED is not available for regions or states does not appear to be a serious problem. Evidence that local wage-setting is based on national price inflation can be seen in the fact reported in *Basic Patterns in Union Contracts* (1983) that just 9 percent of collective bargaining agreements with cost of living adjustments in 1983 used local price indexes in the adjustment formula, while 88 percent used national price indexes. As a result, we present the results with local price indexes only for comparative purpose.

The results presented in this section serve to demonstrate that the two-equation model accurately explains labor market behavior at a finely disaggregated level. The qualitative conclusions drawn from the study

Table 2.4 Fisher Curve Estimates, 16 Large SMSAs, 1964–86

$$U_t^i = \beta_0 + \beta_1 U_{t-1}^i + \beta_2 y_t^i + \beta_3 w_t^i$$

Area	β_0	β_1	β_2	β_3	R^2	h	RESET	Jarque-Bera
New York	−.06	.87	−.21	.45	.93	1.19	0.26	1.24
	(.83)	(.07)	(.08)	(.10)				
Chicago	1.14	.88	−.34	.37	.96	−1.96	1.22	2.03
	(.71)	(.06)	(.05)	(.07)				
Philadelphia	−.30	.88	−.26	.48	.92	−1.86	0.15	1.03
	(.75)	(.07)	(.08)	(.08)				
Detroit	1.38	.89	−.38	.36	.93	−2.97	0.09	0.92
	(.73)	(.06)	(.04)	(.09)				
Boston	.59	.78	−.36	.58	.87	−1.15	0.18	1.17
	(1.01)	(.10)	(.08)	(.16)				
Washington	.76	.82	−.09	.14	.85	−	6.47	0.90
	(.94)	(.12)	(.10)	(.05)				
Pittsburgh	2.44	1.02	−.62	.36	.92	1.76	4.31	0.50
	(1.06)	(.08)	(.11)	(.08)				
St. Louis	.94	.81	−.26	.36	.85	−1.46	0.57	0.02
	(.89)	(.09)	(.08)	(.10)				
Cleveland	1.63	.88	−.38	.33	.90	−.84	0.06	1.80
	(.62)	(.06)	(.06)	(.08)				
Baltimore	4.10	.77	−.47	.27	.88	−	0.16	0.60
	(1.07)	(.08)	(.10)	(.07)				
Dallas– Ft. Worth	1.24	.61	−.20	.37	.79	−	2.40	1.92
	(.92)	(.17)	(.05)	(.10)				
Houston	1.80	.97	−.44	.52	.87	−	5.52	0.75
	(.78)	(.11)	(.06)	(.10)				
Milwaukee	1.08	.94	−.38	.38	.93	−1.60	0.12	0.12
	(.63)	(.06)	(.06)	(.07)				
Minneapolis– St. Paul	1.01	.72	−.22	.34	.80	−11.58	0.34	1.04
	(.70)	(.10)	(.05)	(.07)				
Cincinnati	.07	.88	−.24	.43	.94	−1.20	0.46	0.22
	(1.70)	(.06)	(.05)	(.08)				
Buffalo	.52	.74	−.09	.38	.79	1.78	3.24	0.82
	(1.64)	(.12)	(.18)	(.16)				

Standard errors in parentheses. The h statistic could not be computed for Washington, Baltimore, Dallas–Ft. Worth and Houston. The Durbin–Watson statistics for these areas are, respectively, 1.78, 2.32, 1.74, and 2.34.

Table 2.5 Phillips Curve Estimates, 15 Large SMSAs, 1964–1986, Using Local Price Data

$$w^i = \alpha_0 + \alpha_1 U^i + \alpha_2 p^i_{t-1}$$

Area	α_0	α_1	α_2	R^2	d	RESET	Jarque-Bera
New York	3.36	−.22	.72	.75	2.16	3.17	1.98
	(.60)	(.11)	(.09)				
Chicago	4.29	−.26	.59	.60	1.15	3.32	2.22
	(.76)	(.14)	(.10)				
Philadelphia	4.00	−.10	.53	.53	1.16	.41	1.61
	(.99)	(.20)	(.13)				
Detroit	5.13	−.22	.58	.42	1.30	.77	1.54
	(1.17)	(.16)	(.17)				
Boston	3.81	.14	.29	.48	1.11	7.09	1.27
	(.64)	(.14)	(.08)				
Washington, DC	4.67	−.97	.92	.09	1.30	.67	8.52
	(4.07)	(1.54)	(.55)				
Pittsburgh	5.23	−.53	.77	.52	1.43	1.33	1.45
	(1.64)	(.22)	(.18)				
St. Louis	4.44	−.19	.54	.56	.79	1.13	.32
	(.99)	(.20)	(.11)				
Cleveland	6.01	−.73	.79	.54	1.40	.11	1.30
	(1.22)	(.25)	(.16)				
Baltimore	5.06	−.66	.88	.54	1.02	1.05	1.81
	(1.42)	(.35)	(.19)				
Houston	5.16	−.71	.82	.84	2.39	.41	.98
	(1.05)	(.14)	(.08)				
Milwaukee	5.50	−.65	.75	.83	1.07	3.06	.68
	(.69)	(.14)	(.08)				
Minneapolis–St. Paul	2.96	.04	.54	.59	.90	.24	.61
	(1.10)	(.29)	(.12)				
Cincinnati	3.78	−.22	.69	.52	1.67	2.51	1.25
	(1.06)	(.18)	(.15)				
Buffalo	2.45	.08	.58	.33	1.31	.25	1.73
	(1.55)	(.24)	(.22)				

Estimated using three stage least squares. Standard errors in parentheses.

of the metropolitan areas confirm many of the trends observed when investigating the states. Wages appear to be relatively inflexible in the urban areas of the Northeast, and relatively flexible in the Texan cities; these results mirror the conclusions drawn when analyzing state-level data.

Simulations

In order to illustrate the effect of wage flexibility on regional labor market performance, we have carried out two sets of simulations using the state labor market models reported in tables 2.1 and 2.2. One simulation examines the cyclical behavior of state labor markets by forecasting the wage inflation and unemployment rates in each state for the 1980s under the assumption that state demand growth equaled national GNP growth for each year in that decade. The second simulation assesses the long-run wage inflation and unemployment responses to different growth rates in Gross State Product. Our purpose in this endeavor is to determine if the cyclical and long-run performance of regional labor markets is related to the degree of wage flexibility across the 48 states.

Table 2.6 presents summary statistics from the business cycle simulations for the five states with the highest degree of wage flexibility and the five states with the smallest wage flexibility coefficients. We measure wage flexibility by the negative of α_1, the unemployment coefficient in the Phillips curve. It is important to emphasize that the results in table 2.6 are obtained by using the same values of y and p for each state. Thus the forecasts for the 1980s differ across states only because of differences in the parameters of the Phillips and Fisher curves and because of differences in 1979 unemployment rates.

Some interesting contrasts between the high- and low-wage flexibility states are evident in table 2.6. The simulations indicate that the high-wage flexibility states would have had a slightly lower mean wage inflation rate and a substantially greater variance in wage inflation rates than the low flexibility states under the cyclical conditions represented

**Table 2.6 Summary Statistics for Selected States
of the Results of a Simulation of the 1980s**

	Wage Inflation Mean Variance		Unemployment Mean Variance	
High Flexibility States:				
North Dakota	5.62	9.14	4.69	.06
South Dakota	4.99	9.47	4.21	.16
Nebraska	5.85	7.45	4.13	.34
Utah	5.72	10.21	6.24	.24
Maryland	5.24	8.27	6.13	1.34
Low Flexibility States:				
Rhode Island	6.08	3.38	6.92	2.41
Mississippi	5.90	4.36	9.68	1.34
Massachusetts	6.30	2.70	7.26	.86
New York	6.32	3.55	7.44	1.49
New Jersey	6.20	4.80	8.85	1.24

This simulation involved a dynamic forecast of unemployment and inflation for each year from 1980 to 1989, assuming that state GSP growth was equal to GNP growth.

by national demand growth and consumer price inflation in the United States during the 1980s. Interestingly, the results also predict a lower mean unemployment rate with much smaller annual variation in the unemployment rate for the high-wage flexibility states under the same conditions.

The contrasts evident for the 10 states in table 2.6 are confirmed by correlations across all 48 states. The correlation coefficient between wage flexibility and the mean wage inflation rate generated by the 1980s simulation is $-.43$ while the correlation between wage flexibility and the variance of wage inflation is $+.44$. The correlation coefficients across the 48 states between wage flexibility and the mean and variance of the simulated unemployment rate are $-.56$ and $-.50$, respectively. All four correlation coefficients are statistically significant at the 5 percent level.

The results from this first simulation exercise suggest that states with greater wage flexibility have greater variation in wage inflation rates over the business cycle but, on average, lower wage inflation rates and unemployment rates than states with low degrees of flexibility. There is also an indication that the business cycle, as measured by the variance of the unemployment rate, is less pronounced in states with high degrees of wage flexibility. Obviously the correlations reported here do not prove causation; however, there is evidence that wage flexibility improves labor market performance on a number of important dimensions.

Since the business cycle simulations used the GNP growth rate for all states to facilitate comparisons, we can also use the results of those simulations to ask what would be the effect on local and national unemployment if regional policy were able to equalize the growth of demand across all regions. An answer to that question is presented in table 2.7, which reports simulated and actual unemployment rates for each state for 1982 and 1986. The simulated unemployment rates are those predicted by our labor market model, assuming that demand growth equaled the national average in all states. Thus they give us a clue as to how unemployment rate patterns might respond to a redistribution of demand from high-growth states to slow-growth states.

The results of this exercise indicate that such a redistribution would have fairly large effects on individual states and census regions. For example, growth at the national average would have resulted in significantly higher unemployment rates for all the northeastern states except Pennsylvania in both 1982 and 1986. In contrast, lower unemployment rates would have been registered in most of the Central states if regional demand growth had increased at a pace equivalent to the rate of growth of GNP. This is certainly consistent with the perception of a sharp disparity in economic performance during the 1980s between the East Coast and the heartland of the country.

An interesting pattern emerges in the results reported for the West South Central and Mountain regions. For most of these states, demand growth at the national rate would have resulted in higher unemployment rates in 1982 and lower rates in 1986. This largely reflects changes in the markets for oil and other raw materials affecting the growth in Gross State Product in these regions. Finally, the results for the South Atlantic

**Table 2.7   A Comparison of Actual Unemployment Rates
to Those Forecast Under the Assumption of Uniform Demand Growth
Across all States, 1982 and 1986**

	1982		1986	
	Forecast	Actual	Forecast	Actual
New England				
Maine	10.8	8.6	7.7	5.3
New Hampshire	9.6	7.4	7.8	2.8
Vermont	8.4	6.9	6.8	4.7
Massachusetts	9.0	7.9	7.4	3.8
Connecticut	8.3	6.9	7.8	3.8
Rhode Island	9.9	10.2	6.2	4.0
Middle Atlantic				
Pennsylvania	10.2	10.9	6.7	6.8
New York	9.0	8.6	6.9	6.3
New Jersey	10.9	9.0	9.0	5.0
East North Central				
Ohio	10.1	12.5	7.0	8.1
Indiana	9.7	11.9	6.2	6.7
Illinois	9.1	11.3	6.8	8.1
Michigan	11.9	15.5	8.3	8.8
Wisconsin	9.0	10.4	6.1	7.0
West North Central				
Minnesota	7.0	7.8	5.2	5.3
Iowa	7.0	8.5	5.3	7.0
Missouri	8.1	9.2	6.2	6.1
North Dakota	4.8	5.9	4.1	6.3
South Dakota	4.8	5.5	4.1	4.7
Nebraska	5.2	6.1	3.9	5.0
Kansas	6.2	6.3	4.6	5.4
South Atlantic				
Delaware	9.7	8.5	5.2	4.3
Maryland	8.2	8.4	5.4	4.5
Virginia	7.8	7.7	5.5	5.5
West Virginia	12.2	13.9	8.6	11.8
North Carolina	9.4	9.0	7.2	5.3
South Carolina	9.7	10.8	6.2	7.5
Georgia	9.0	7.8	8.9	5.9
Florida	10.4	8.2	7.0	5.7

Table 2.7 (*continued*)

| | 1982 | | 1986 | |
	Forecast	Actual	Forecast	Actual
East South Central				
Kentucky	9.7	10.6	7.5	9.3
Tennessee	10.7	11.8	8.2	8.0
Alabama	12.7	13.7	9.9	9.8
Mississippi	11.3	11.0	9.9	11.7
West South Central				
Arkansas	10.0	9.8	7.5	8.7
Louisiana	10.8	10.3	9.5	13.1
Oklahoma	8.9	5.7	5.2	8.2
Texas	9.1	6.9	6.5	8.9
Mountain				
Montana	7.4	8.6	6.6	8.6
Idaho	8.5	9.8	6.8	8.7
Wyoming	6.8	5.8	5.0	9.0
Colorado	8.2	7.7	5.4	7.4
New Mexico	10.6	9.2	7.3	9.2
Arizona	10.8	9.9	7.6	6.9
Utah	7.2	7.8	6.2	6.0
Nevada	10.6	10.1	7.8	10.1
Pacific				
Washington	11.5	12.1	9.1	8.2
Oregon	10.7	11.5	7.8	8.5
California	8.6	9.9	10.0	6.7
Weighted Average	9.4	9.7	7.4	7.0

and Pacific regions are mixed, with some states benefitting and others losing from an equalization of demand growth.

When the state unemployment rates are averaged using labor force weights, we see that demand growth equalization would have had a minor effect on the national unemployment rate. The simulated rate for 1982 is 0.3 points lower and that for 1986 0.4 points higher than the actual rates for those years. This suggests the possibility that eliminating regional disparities in demand growth might smooth out slightly the

50

Table 2.8   Demand Growth Multipliers, Selected States

	Wage Inflation	Unemployment
High Flexibility States:		
North Dakota	.26	−.09
South Dakota	.22	−.09
Nebraska	.39	−.26
Utah	.34	−.18
Maryland	.55	−.38
Low Flexibility States:		
Rhode Island	.26	−.72
Mississippi	.31	−.84
Massachusetts	.16	−1.23
New York	.06	−.66
New Jersey	.12	−1.52

The multipliers equal the difference between 1991 dynamic forecasts assuming $y=8\%$ and $p=5\%$ for each year from 1987 to 1991 and 1991 forecasts assuming $y=7\%$ and $p=5\%$ for each year from 1987 to 1991.

cyclical pattern of unemployment rates at the national level while having fairly large impacts on individual states. A more complete model, expanded to include the determination of regional price inflation, would be necessary to study the effects of demand growth equalization on national inflation. The estimation of such a model would require new data on regional prices.

Our second set of simulations addresses the longer-term effect of demand growth on unemployment rates and wage inflation. To estimate this we developed two sets of forecasts for each state for the 1987-1991 period. The first assumed $y=8$ percent and $p=5$ percent for each state in each of those years and the second assumed $y=7$ percent and $p=5$ percent for each of those years. From the 1991 forecasts derived in this manner, we can calculate "multipliers" measuring the effect of 8 percent demand growth versus 7 percent demand growth on wage inflation and unemployment. Such multipliers are reported in table 2.8 for the states at the high and low end of the wage flexibility spectrum.

The results in table 2.8 suggest that the unemployment rate impact of faster demand growth is substantially higher for the low-wage flexibility states. Across all 48 states, the correlation coefficient between wage flexibility and the unemployment multiplier, measured in absolute value terms, is .55. Interestingly, there is no significant correlation ($r = .24$) between wage flexibility and the wage inflation multiplier. The results from this growth simulation need to be considered with particular care since migration responses, which are neglected by our model, are likely to be more important over longer time horizons.

Conclusions

Economists brought up in the neoclassical tradition have strong ideas about what constitutes a perfect world. Information is complete, transactions and mobility are costless, restrictions on economic activity are absent, and markets exist for everything. Within such a perfect world, the operation of an economy is well understood; outside it, controversy persists. Disagreements therefore arise frequently when markets do not (appear to) work. Surpluses and gluts are blemishes; they may cure themselves quickly, or they may indicate that treatment is required (either to restore perfect market conditions or to compensate for chronically imperfect ones).

Unemployment occurs when the market for labor fails to clear a surplus. Its persistence is therefore a source of much disagreement among economists. The sluggish supply-side behavior embodied in the traditional (short-run) Phillips curve matches the eclectic Keynesian view of markets which do not always clear. According to this model, a tradeoff exists (in the short run at least) between inflation and unemployment. Such a view has faced a stern challenge over the last 20 years, both from the theoretical advances achieved by the new classical school and from the empirical observation of worldwide stagflation in the wake of the oil shocks of the seventies. As a result, naive models of the Phillips curve have been swept aside, to be replaced by more sophisticated systems. It has become clear that when changes in price expectations influence labor supply decisions (and so buffet about the Phillips curve), the path pursued by the economy depends also on the shape of aggregate demand. The wage-employment solution arrived at in any period depends, therefore, on both aggregate supply and aggregate demand conditions.

In this chapter, the simultaneous determination of wage inflation and unemployment has been captured by way of a simple two-equation model. The first equation is the familiar expectations-augmented Phillips curve. This is based on the optimal response to labor market conditions and expected price changes on the part of workers supplying labor services. The second equation derives from the early work of Irving Fisher, and represents the unemployment effects of changes on the demand side of the economy; we have called this the Fisher curve. Together, the Phillips and Fisher curves describe the movement of wage inflation and unemployment rates over the business cycle.

When applying an identical model to a large number of small economies, some problems and local idiosyncracies are sure to arise. It has been a matter of surprise to us that so few difficulties have arisen out of our choice of an exceedingly simple model. In the large majority of states and metropolitan areas, the model works very satisfactorily indeed. The coefficients have the signs and magnitudes predicted by theory, and the model passes a tough series of diagnostic tests designed to highlight statistical difficulties. In the few states and cities where statistical problems were identified, these have been bypassed using standard methods. For these areas, the corrected functions once more produce reasonable coefficient estimates and a good fit to the data. The within-sample predictive power of the model is good in all states and cities and, while the data series are not sufficiently long to allow rigorous testing of out-of-sample properties, our work on national data (Hyclak and Johnes 1990) indicates that the model works well in this respect too.

Of central interest in the context of this book is the coefficient on unemployment in the state-specific Phillips curves. This enables us to derive a measure of wage flexibility which will be used extensively in the next chapter as we seek to establish the determinants of wage rigidity. A quick glance at the unemployment coefficients of the state-specific Phillips curves is sufficient to establish that spatial variation in wage flexibility is present. Some broad trends are immediately apparent. Wages tend to be less flexible in the Northeast than elsewhere, and are especially flexible in the northern plains and the Pacific Northwest. A more detailed consideration of these patterns will form the basis of the next chapter.

3

Inter-Regional Differences in Wage Flexibility

A glance at figure 2.1 reinforces a central conclusion of the preceding chapter: the unemployment responsiveness of manufacturing wage inflation varies quite considerably across the 48 states. The purpose of this chapter is to attempt an empirical explanation of these interstate differences in wage flexibility.

Our method follows that of Kaun and Spiro (1970) and Grubb, Jackman, and Layard (1983) in using the state-specific estimates of the unemployment coefficient from the Phillips curve as the dependent variable in a cross-section analysis. Our sample of 48 states allows for considerably more degrees of freedom than these previous studies and gives us the advantage of conducting a cross-section analysis within a common legal and regulatory environment, unlike studies of international differences in wage flexibility. The independent variables in the cross-section analysis are derived from hypotheses developed in recent theoretical models of wage rigidity.

This chapter is organized in the following manner. The first section presents a brief review of recent theories of wage rigidity, followed by a definition of the specific hypotheses and variables we will test in the cross-state regressions and discussion of data sources. Results of the basic regression analysis are presented in the third section and in the fourth we extend the cross-section model to consider simultaneous equations issues. The chapter concludes with a brief summary of the results.

Theories of Wage Rigidity

Given the central importance of wage and price rigidity in most macroeconomic models, it is not surprising that there has been a considerable number of theories of wage rigidity offered in the literature in recent years. Two broad approaches can be identified: The new classical economics emphasizes an equilibrium approach which treats apparent wage rigidity as the result of "flat" labor supply curves reflecting intertemporal labor-leisure tradeoffs, transactions costs, or changes in the reservation wage of marginal workers. An alternative method has been to emphasize the various characteristics of labor markets that generate significant and persistent disequilibrium wage outcomes. Careful reviews of wage rigidity theories by Kniesner and Goldsmith (1987) and Blanchard and Fischer (1989) cast considerable doubt on the applicability of the equilibrium approach to understanding why labor demand shocks affect employment to a much greater degree than wages. As a result, three related disequilibrium theories, which have received considerable attention in recent years, will be the focus of our empirical analysis of interstate differences in wage flexibility. These are contract theory, efficiency wage theory and the insider-outsider theory. In addition to reviewing each of these theories below, we also examine the way in which state labor policies might affect wage flexibility.

Contract Theory

Here we refer to two separate theories: the implicit contract theory, first formalized by Azariadis (1975) and Baily (1974), and the theory of staggered, overlapping union contracts developed by Okun (1981) and Taylor (1979). In both cases, wages are rigid in the face of a labor market shock because they have been contractually fixed. In the simple implicit contract theory, firms and workers are viewed as entering into voluntary agreements in which risk-neutral firms guarantee risk-averse workers a degree of income stability in the face of uncertainty about the future state of labor demand. These unwritten contracts may result in steady real wages regardless of the level of labor demand, with workers paying for such real wage insurance by accepting a lower average real wage over time than would be generated by a competitive labor market. While this theory offers an explanation for wage rigidity, it falters in its implications for employment changes and does not provide an explanation for the absence of contingency contracts that offer stable employment levels. A second version of implicit contract theory (Grossman and Hart 1981) relies on the assumption that the firm has better information about the state of the labor market and, hence, has the opportunity to gain by misrepresenting the true state. Under this condition, risk-averse workers gain by an implicit contract fixing the real wage and letting the firm choose employment.

Implicit contract theory has been criticized because it provides a rationale for fixed income contracts rather than the fixed-wage variable employment contracts that seem to dominate the labor market (Gordon 1990a) and because it fails to explain the less than full indexation of wages observed in the economy (Kniesner and Goldsmith 1987). However, it is a practical matter that makes this theory of little use in our analysis of the determinants of interstate differences in wage rigidity. While it is possible that states differ in the extent to which workers and firms enter into wage-fixing implicit contracts, the theory provides no guidance as to how this might be measured in practice. This is amply illustrated by the fact that such contracts are not written and are somehow reached by consensus without explicit negotiations. And it is difficult to conceive of appropriate statistical counterparts to the degree of risk aversion and information asymmetries in a regional labor market. Thus, while the theory provides a rationale for the existence of observed wage rigidity, it does not provide an operational hypothesis to use in our analysis.

The second contract-based theory of wage rigidity starts from the observation that in the union sector of the U.S. labor market contracts are generally negotiated at the plant level, usually are in effect for more than one year, have staggered starting and ending dates, and specify periodic wage adjustments, often explicitly linked to price inflation, over the contract life. Rigidity is built into union wages by the inertia created when some portion of current nominal wage adjustments are affected by expectations and labor market conditions prevailing during contract negotiations a year or more in the past. Employment instability results from unexpected price inflation or demand shocks during the term of the multiyear contract. Card's (1990) study of union contracts in

Canada provides considerable empirical support for these hypotheses. He found that nominal wage contracting in multiyear pacts led to unexpected changes in real wages that played an important role in explaining cyclical movements in union employment. He also found that unexpected real wage changes tended to be carried over into the next agreement, suggesting that inertia in the union sector may prevail over several contract periods.

Union contract theory takes as given the institutional framework for collective bargaining in the United States and does not explain why contracts set wage levels rather than employment or why wages are not linked to the performance of the firm or the economy in a way that stabilizes employment (Gordon 1990a). And in the United States, unions represent a fairly small fraction of the workforce. Still, the potential importance of wage rigidity caused by union contracts suggests that some measure of union activity be included among the independent variables in our cross-section analysis. This conclusion is also indicated by the empirical studies of Kaun and Spiro (1970), who found a negative relationship between an index of union density and the unemployment coefficient from time series Phillips curve estimates in a cross-section of 30 metropolitan areas, and Mitchell (1980), whose results showed significantly lower wage flexibility in more heavily unionized industries. Thus, one hypothesis for this chapter is that the extent of union contract coverage will be negatively related to wage flexibility across the states.

Efficiency Wage Theory

The basic hypothesis of efficiency wage theory is that firms may find it advantageous to pay wages in excess of market-clearing levels if worker efficiency is positively related to compensation. More important for our purposes, efficiency considerations would lead a firm to resist cutting wages even in the face of substantial excess labor supply because cutting wages might lower productivity and actually raise labor costs. Katz's (1986) review of the efficiency wage literature identified five distinct, yet complementary, explanations for a positive relationship between worker efficiency and the wage level:

(1) Paying above-market wages raises the cost of losing a job and hence acts as a deterrent to shirking in jobs where close monitoring of worker performance is impossible.

(2) Efficiency wages lower turnover costs to the extent that they result in lower quit rates and increased tenure.

(3) Paying above market wages serves to increase the overall quality of the pool of job applicants, and maintaining wage levels in a downturn lowers the risk of losing the firm's best, most mobile workers.

(4) If the wage standard is perceived to be fair, then greater worker morale and loyalty might enhance effort and productivity and facilitate teamwork.

(5) Higher than required wages may be used to secure industrial peace in unionized establishments or to forestall union organization in nonunion firms.

The appeal of efficiency wage theory is that it not only provides an explanation for wage rigidity and employment variability over the business cycle, but it also yields results that are consistent with a number of labor market situations that have proven anomalous for competitive labor theory. For example, if the conditions leading to efficiency wage gains vary with the size, technology, or profitability of the firm, then efficiency wage considerations can be used to explain the existence of wage differentials across firms or industries for similar workers. And efficiency wage theory is consistent with the observed dual nature of U.S. labor markets, with a sector of competitive low-wage employers, for whom efficiency wage factors may not be important, coexisting with a sector of employers paying high wages and providing long-term career opportunities.

While it is safe to say that efficiency wage theory has had a great appeal to many economists in recent years, there have been several criticisms leveled against this approach. The recent papers by Carmichael (1990) and Lang and Kahn (1990) present a detailed discussion of the pros and cons of the theory. To summarize, there appear to be three main critiques: First, it is argued that the wage is performing both an allocative and an incentive task in efficiency wage theory, and that other mechanisms, such as performance bonuses, piece rates, or tournaments, would perform better in regulating the intensity of work effort. The absence of widespread use of such mechanisms appears to call into question the importance of efficiency considerations. Second, since a prominent version of efficiency wage theory relies partially on the threat of unemployment as a deterrent to shirking, it is argued that the theory cannot explain involuntary unemployment since such unemployment is assumed to be exogenous in the formulation of a firm's wage policy (Barro 1989). And third, it is argued that efficiency wage theory alone cannot fully explain wage rigidity without being coupled with an explicit recognition of the coordination problems inherent in reducing wages at one firm when relative wages are important (Gordon 1990a).

Thus far the empirical evidence on the efficiency wage hypothesis has been mostly indirect (Krueger and Summers 1988). However, a recent paper by Blinder and Choi (1990) reports the results of a small interview survey of personnel managers and many of their findings seem to be consistent with the efficiency wage hypothesis. In particular, a large proportion of the managers interviewed agreed that wage cuts would lower work effort, increase quits, and impose significant hiring and training costs on the firm. And there seemed to be general agreement that the firm risked significant costs from being perceived as pursuing an "unfair" wage policy. A second hypothesis to consider in our analysis, then, is that wage flexibility will be negatively related to the relative importance of efficiency wage policies across the states.

Insider-Outsider Theory

The insider-outsider theory, developed principally by Lindbeck and Snower (1988), has received considerable attention as an explanation for wage and price rigidity in the face of extremely high unemployment rates in most European countries during the 1980s. This hypothesis starts with the idea that insiders, currently employed or temporarily laid-off workers, are imperfect substitutes for outsiders, those who have not recently worked for the firm. Thus it may not be profitable for a firm to hire unemployed workers at lower wages because of an array of firing, hiring, and training costs. These costs enable insiders, especially when represented by unions, to extract a rent from the employer in the form of higher than competitive wages that generally are cyclically inflexible. Unemployment results even though outsiders are willing to accept jobs at lower wages than insiders as long as the wage differential paid to insiders does not exceed the turnover costs. In addition to offering an explanation for wage rigidity and involuntary unemployment, insider-outsider theory has been used to explain hysteresis in the equilibrium unemployment rate. A shock that lowers employment and increases the number of outsiders may lead to an increase in the equilibrium unemployment rate if wage levels are predominantly determined in the best interest of the employed insiders rather than reflecting excess supply conditions in the labor market as a whole.

Krueger and Summers (1988, p.280) regard the insider-outsider model as "...a species of efficiency wage theory rather than as an alternative explanation for wage differentials." Therefore, many of the criticisms outlined above also apply to this model. In addition, the theory provides no clear rationale why two-tier wage systems, in which above-market wages are paid to insiders and market-level wages are paid to new hires, would not be employed. The widespread use of such systems along with concession bargaining in the United States in the 1980s (Flanagan 1984) would seem to call into question some of the basic tenets of insider-outsider theory, at least as applied to the United States. However, there are two specific hypotheses derived from the insider-outsider model that need to be included in our analysis of interstate differences in wage flexibility. The first hypothesis is that wage flexibility is inversely related to the extent of long-term unemployment. The argument here is that workers who have been unemployed for long periods of time undergo a deterioration in their skills that makes them outsiders from the point of view of firm wage policy. The second hypothesis is that wage inflation is more responsive to changes in unemployment via layoffs than to the level of unemployment. This is because unions are responsive to both the wage and employment prospects of their members and are more likely to moderate wage demands when faced with an increase in job losses for their members.

The notion that layoffs might have a bigger impact on wage adjustments than the level of unemployment also seems to fit efficiency wage models based on the relationship between work effort and the perceived fairness of wages (Akerlof and Yellen 1990). The survey results of Blinder and Choi (1990) indicated agreement among personnel managers that wage cuts in response to decreased labor demand could be implemented without an adverse effort response if such cuts could be justified to the workers as fair. Such justification could be based on the need to align wages with those of competitors, since wage comparisons are likely to be a major criterion in assessing fairness, or the need to help the firm weather a particularly serious competitive threat.

Public Policy

Chan-Lee, Coe, and Prywes (1987) examine a number of government policies that potentially affect the responsiveness of labor markets to economic shocks. They cite four general types of government policies in this regard: minimum wage levels, unemployment compensation replacement and coverage rates, public sector pay policies, and general regulations of labor relations. They find no empirical evidence to support the notion that liberalization of such policies, which has happened in a number of European countries during the 1980s, had a significant effect on the responsiveness of wage inflation to unemployment. Still, our cross-state analysis considers the impact of three policy variables on wage flexibility.

The minimum wage can affect wage flexibility by insulating the wages of covered workers from market forces. In a cross-state analysis, those regions where minimum wages are relatively more important should exhibit greater wage rigidity. However, it has been argued that in the United States the labor market effect of the minimum wage has been limited because the vast majority of workers earn wages in excess of the minimum level, there are substantial gaps in coverage, the real value of the minimum wage drops considerably in years between legislated changes, and there is substantial employer noncompliance (Brown 1988). Our empirical analysis addresses the effect of the minimum wage on wage flexibility by including a measure of the relative minimum wage in the regressions.

While Katz (1986) argues that the level and availability of unemployment insurance benefits might have an effect on the level of efficiency wages required to inhibit shirking, there is no clear hypothesis in the literature to suggest that unemployment insurance would directly affect the responsiveness of wage inflation to unemployment. Such benefits may have an indirect impact, however, given the evidence of significant unemployment compensation effects on the willingness of firms to use temporary layoffs (Topel 1983) and on the duration of unemployment (Ehrenberg and Oaxaca 1976). In addition, research by Katz (1977) and Johnson, Dickinson and West (1985) suggests that referrals from the Public Employment Service may act to reduce the duration of unemployment by shortening the period of job search for some workers. We examine the indirect effect of the unemployment insurance and public employment systems in the simultaneous equations model discussed later in this chapter.

As a measure of the overall public policy toward labor-management relations in a state, we focus on whether or not a state has adopted a "right-to-work" law. While the literal significance of these laws is that unions are prohibited from negotiating compulsory membership requirements into collective agreements, their true significance lies as an indicator of the overall "bias" in state policy regarding labor-management relations. In this regard, right-to-work laws are often used in measures of the "business climate" of a state. A recent survey of the literature on right-to-work laws by Moore and Newman (1985) indicates that there is some evidence, although not overwhelming evidence, that such laws, or the tastes of the citizenry reflected through such laws, have the effect of reducing union membership and bargaining power. Since union bargaining power plays an important role in contract theory and the insider-outsider hypothesis, it might be expected that greater wage flexibility would be observed in states affected by right-to-work laws.

In summary, our reading of the recent theoretical approaches to explaining wage flexibility suggests the following hypotheses: (1) wage flexibility will be lower in states where a greater proportion of workers are covered by union contracts; (2) wage flexibility will be lower in states where employers make greater use of efficiency wages; (3) wage flexibility will be lower in states with a larger fraction of long-term unemployed workers; and (4) wage flexibility will be higher in states with a larger fraction of the unemployed on temporary layoff. In addition, we expect greater flexibility in right-to-work states and in states where minimum wages are less important.

Our study of wage inflation and unemployment in the 10 economic regions of Great Britain (Hyclak and Johnes 1992) lends some support to a couple of these hypotheses. We found that an index of wage flexibility was negatively correlated with the proportion of working days lost through work stoppages and with the percent of the labor force out of work for over a year across the 10 regions. However, the small sample of regions in that study limited the analysis to an examination of correlations.

One result from our study of the British regions that could not be replicated in initial runs in this study concerns the effect of labor market mismatch. A mismatch between the skills required for vacancies and those possessed by the unemployed might reduce wage flexibility in a manner analogous to that hypothesized for the long-term unemployed. In our study of the regions in Great Britain, we found evidence of a negative correlation between wage flexibility and Layard and Nickell's (1986) measure of mismatch resulting from changes in industrial structure. However, neither that variable nor a measure of occupational mismatch developed by Jackman, Layard and Savouri (1990) were ever statistically significant in regressions for the states. This may be due to greater mobility in the United States, to greater variation in the relative performance of various regions in the United States over time, or to the difficulties of measuring mismatch. Since it is difficult to disentangle labor market mismatch from the insider-outsider effects, we have excluded the mismatch variables from the regression results reported below.

Determinants of Wage Flexibility

In this section we define the variables used in the cross-section regression analysis of interstate differences in the responsiveness of wage inflation to unemployment. The dependent variable in these regressions is the negative of the unemployment coefficient in the Phillips curve regressions reported in table 2.1. This measure of wage responsiveness to labor market slack is highly correlated with all of the other Phillips curve unemployment coefficients discussed in chapter 2 and in the appendix. For convenience we name the dependent variable WFLEX for the rest of this chapter.

One measure of interstate differences in the extent to which firms utilize efficiency wages is based on the interindustry estimates of Krueger and Summers (1988). They examined the industry wage structure and estimated the proportionate difference in wages between an employee in a given industry and the average employee, controlling for human capital variables, occupation, and union status. The effects of industry affiliation on relative wages in their study is quite pronounced – changing industry had about the same impact as changing union status – and remarkably stable across space and time (see also Krueger and Summers 1987). They carefully eliminated a number of competing explanations for these industry wage effects and concluded that they represented differences in the use of efficiency wages. Since they found their estimates to be stable across geographic regions, we use the Krueger and Summers estimates to construct a measure of the efficiency wage industry mix (EWMIX) for each state in 1974. The efficiency wage industry mix is defined as the weighted average across 6 one-digit nonmanufacturing industries and 20 two-digit manufacturing industries of the national industry wage effects, using the proportion of state employment in each industry as weights. To the extent that this variable captures interstate differences in efficiency wage use, we expect the efficiency wage industry mix to be negatively related to wage flexibility.

A second variable related to the efficiency wage hypothesis is the proportion of establishments in each state with 20 or fewer employees

(SMALL). Small establishments are less likely to employ efficiency wage systems because it is easier to monitor the work effort of individuals in small firms and because small firms generally are less able to afford to pay wages above the market level (Groshen 1988 and Brown 1990). Ehrenberg and Smith (1991) suggest also that the significantly higher turnover registered by small firms means that at any given time a relatively large proportion of these firms are new entrants with no established wage structure who are better able to scale wages to market levels. Thus we expect SMALL to be positively related to wage flexibility. Data on the fraction of establishments with 20 or fewer workers are from the 1977 *County Business Patterns*.

The data published by the Department of Labor in the annual *Geographic Profile of Employment and Unemployment* allow us to construct variables measuring state differences in the importance of long-term unemployment and temporary layoffs. Since any definition of "long term" is inherently arbitrary, we employ two measures of long-term unemployment. LTU26 is the percentage of the unemployed who were out of work for more than 26 weeks in a given year. Data are available on LTU26 for the 11 years from 1976 to 1986. In order to control for cyclical effects, LTU26 for each state is calculated as the mean value over that time span. We also use a measure of the fraction of the unemployed out of work for more than 52 weeks (LTU52). Data for this variable are available only for the six years from 1976 to 1981 and again LTU52 for each state is calculated as the mean over that period. Data are also available on the percentage of the unemployed who were on layoff in each state for 1976 and 1981 to 1986. The variable LAYOFF is the average of that fraction for each state for the available years. The discussion in the previous section suggests that long-term unemployment should be negatively related to wage flexibility while layoff unemployment is expected to have a positive effect on wage flexibility.

To measure the extent of union coverage (UNION) we use the estimates of the percentage of employees who were union members in each state by Troy and Sheflin (1985). They report union density figures for each state for the years 1960, 1975, 1980 and 1982. UNION is calculated as the mean value for each state for these four years. Troy and Sheflin were also the source for information on states with right-to-work laws (RTW). UNION should have a negative effect and RTW a positive effect on wage flexibility. The relative minimum wage was calculated for each state by dividing the statutory minimum wage by the average hourly wage in manufacturing for the years 1964 to 1986. RELMIN is defined as the mean relative minimum wage for each state over that span of years. The minimum wage is likely to have a stronger impact on states with high values for RELMIN and, hence, we expect this variable to be negatively related to WFLEX.

Table 3.1 provides the means, standard deviations, and ranges for each of the variables used in our analysis of the determinants of wage flexibility across the 48 states in the sample. The mean value for our efficiency wage – industrial mix variable is negative because of the relatively large weight given to retail, wholesale, and services employment in most states and the negative industry wage effects for these industries in Krueger and Summers (1988). States at the low end of the range for EWMIX are Maine, Nebraska, North Dakota, South Dakota and Rhode Island, while Iowa, Michigan, West Virginia, and Delaware join Wyoming at the high end. There does not appear to be any clear regional pattern to the values of EWMIX. The data for the fraction of establishments accounted for by small firms runs in a fairly narrow range across the states. The lowest values are for older, industrial states like Ohio, Massachusetts, Maryland, and Illinois while the highest values are seen in more rural states like Maine, Montana, and North and South Dakota. A similar pattern holds with the relative minimum wage. In this case, Washington and Oregon join the industrial states of Michigan and Ohio at the low end of the range. North and South Carolina, Mississippi, and Arkansas register the highest values for RELMIN. Layoffs and long-term unemployment seem more prominent in the industrial northeast and less so in the mountain states. The cross-state pattern of UNION and RTW is quite familiar, with greater unionization in the industrial states.

Single Equation Estimates

Table 3.2 presents the results of several regressions of WFLEX on the independent variables across the sample of 48 states. Since the depen-

**Table 3.1 Descriptive Statistics on Variables
Used in the Cross-Section Analysis**

Variable	Mean	Standard Deviation	Low	High
WFLEX	.7766	.5601	−.1212(NM)	2.9000(ND)
EWMIX	−.0092	.0123	−.0328(NV)	.0248(WY)
SMALL	.8872	.0133	.8604(IL)	.9209(MT)
UNION	.2250	.0868	.0613(SC)	.4166(MI)
RTW	.4166	.4982	0	1.0
RELMIN	.4540	.0655	.3374(MI)	.5922(NC)
LAYOFF	.1552	.0541	.0634(NM)	.2756(PA)
LTU26	.1356	.0383	.0695(WY)	.2250(WV)
LTU52	.0468	.0196	.0115(WY)	.1025(NY)

dent variable in these regressions is itself a regression coefficient, the variance of WFLEX differs substantially from state to state and is likely to be proportional to the residual variance in an ordinary least squares (OLS) regression. Thus we report both ordinary least squares and generalized least squares (GLS) estimates. In the GLS regressions, the inverse of the variance of WFLEX from the time series results is used to weight the observations for each state (see Granger et al. 1979 and Kaun and Spiro 1970). And the OLS results report the heteroskedasticity − consistent standard errors from the method of White (1980). In general, the results are very good. The regressions explain a fairly high proportion of the state-to-state variation in wage flexibility and the tests for specification error and normality are acceptable. The independent variables are generally statistically significant, with the expected signs indicating considerable support for the hypotheses derived from the efficiency wage and insider-outsider theories of wage rigidity.

The efficiency wage industry mix variable has a statistically significant negative relationship with WFLEX in all four regressions reported in table 3.1. The indication is that states with fewer employees in industries employing efficiency wage schemes, as measured by Krueger and Summers (1988), also have greater wage flexibility. The efficiency wage link to wage rigidity is also supported by the statistically signifi-

Table 3.2   Determinants of Interstate Differences in Wage Flexibility

	OLS	OLS	GLS	GLS
CONSTANT	−7.23	−3.34	−8.14	−8.88
	(4.46)	(4.48)	(5.04)	(5.16)
EWMIX	−24.28	−23.84	−39.06	−38.90
	(6.95)	(6.83)	(4.84)	(4.97)
	[−.53]	[−.52]	[−.86]	[−.86]
SMALL	12.88	8.04	14.01	14.82
	(4.88)	(5.14)	(5.15)	(5.36)
	[.30]	[.19]	[.33]	[.35]
UNION	−4.26	−2.96	−5.75	−6.14
	(1.78)	(1.57)	(2.00)	(1.90)
	[−.66]	[−.46]	[−.89]	[−.95]
RTW	0.53	0.50	0.64	0.64
	(0.17)	(0.17)	(0.17)	(0.18)
	[.47]	[.44]	[.56]	[.56]
RELMIN	−7.80	−6.68	−8.04	−8.20
	(1.84)	(1.80)	(2.30)	(2.31)
	[−.91]	[−.78]	[−.94]	[−.96]
LAYOFF	2.85	3.58	7.21	6.99
	(1.12)	(1.04)	(1.87)	(1.88)
	[.27]	[.35]	[.70]	[.68]
LTU26	1.40		−2.26	
	(1.96)		(3.40)	
	[.09]		[−.15]	
LTU52		−6.32		−1.78
		(3.17)		(6.02)
		[−.22]		[−.06]
$\bar{R}^2$	.50	.52	.89	.89
RESET	0.85	1.30	2.21	2.51
JARQUE-BERA	1.34	2.62	0.93	1.16

Parentheses contain standard errors. For the OLS regressions we report the heteroskedasticity-consistent standard errors of White (1980). Beta coefficients are reported in brackets. GLS estimates weight each observation by the inverse of the estimated variance of WFLEX.

cant positive coefficients on SMALL, indicating greater wage flexibility in states with a higher proportion of employment in firms with fewer than 20 employees. To the extent that small firms do not face the same monitoring costs that make efficient wage mechanisms profitable, this result is also consistent with the hypothesis that the use of efficiency wages affects overall wage flexibility.

It is possible to interpret the results for these two variables as consistent with implicit contract theory. Such theory is likely to apply more readily to employment situations involving long-term attachments and specific training. Such situations are likely to vary across firms and industries and EWMIX and SMALL may be capturing such effects. And the size effect may reflect heterogeneity in skills, capital intensity, and technology across firms as well as greater product market competition among small firms in addition to contract and efficiency wages effects. These results provide only an indirect test of the efficiency wage hypothesis and might more generously be interpreted as evidence for other theories which explain stable interindustry wage differentials, despite Krueger and Summers' (1988) valiant effort to rule out alternative explanations for their measures.

The union density variable has a statistically significant negative coefficient in all four regressions reported in table 3.1. This is consistent with the earlier finding of Kaun and Spiro (1970) and with the hypothesis that collective bargaining agreements contribute to overall wage rigidity. The importance of the labor relations climate in explaining state-by-state differences in wage flexibility is evidenced by the significant positive coefficients estimated for RTW. The results also indicate that wage flexibility is significantly lower in states where the minimum wage is relatively more important.

Mixed results are registered for the two variables suggested by the insider-outsider theory of wage determination. The estimated coefficient on LAYOFF is highly significant and positive, indicating greater wage flexibility in states where a higher fraction of the unemployed were on temporary layoff in the mid-1970s and early 1980s. This is consistent with the notion that the responsiveness of wages to overall unemployment levels is sensitive to the composition of unemployment by cause, which can be explained by unions taking into account the threat of job loss to current employees in setting wage demands but, as is suggested by the insider-outsider theory, not responding as readily to search unemployment by job quitters or labor force entrants. This result for LAYOFF is also what might be expected from a reading of the literature on the appearance of substantial union wage concessions in the 1980s (Wachter and Carter 1989). On the other hand, long-term unemployment generally is not a statistically significant determinant of wage flexibility, except in the case of LTU52 in the second OLS regression. This is in contrast to a number of European studies and our own results in analysing wage flexibility across the 10 economic regions of Great Britain. It may be that the combination of more vigorous job creation and less generous unemployment compensation makes long-term unemployment less serious in the United States than in Europe. In addition, this result might reflect the relatively low variation in long-term unemployment across the 48 states.

Beta coefficients, shown in brackets in table 3.2, can be used to measure the relative strength of the independent variables in affecting the dependent variable. No single independent variable is revealed as a dominant determinant of wage flexibility across the states. Unionization, the relative minimum wage, and the efficiency wage industry mix have the strongest effects in both the OLS and GLS regressions. The average fraction of the unemployed on layoff has a much higher beta coefficient in the GLS regressions. The right-to-work law dummy has consistent effects across the regressions that are only slightly weaker than those for the other variables. The fraction of establishments with 20 or fewer workers and long-term unemployment seem to have relatively small effects on wage flexibility, by this measure.

Concentrating on the GLS estimates, we see that a one standard deviation increase in EWMIX, UNION and RELMIN is associated with close to a one standard deviation decrease in our wage flexibility measure. The strong effect noted for the relative minimum wage variable reflects largely the impact of regional wage structure on flexibility, since the source of cross-state variation in RELMIN is the average manufacturing wage. A one standard deviation increase in LAYOFF and RTW is associated with a .70 and .56 standard deviation rise in flexibility. Clearly, these variables are also important determinants of cross-state differences in wage flexibility.

Wage flexibility is highest in the West North Central region and in North and South Dakota, in particular. These states have relatively low unionization rates, right-to-work laws, a high proportion of small firms and relatively low efficiency wage industry mixes. The opposite description on these four measures characterizes the industrial states in the East North Central, Middle Atlantic and New England states where wage flexibility is relatively low. Differences in LAYOFF between these areas are also quite pronounced.

Wage flexibility is surprisingly low for a number of southern states where unionization is not important and right-to-work laws exist. This is especially the case for Georgia, Alabama, Tennessee, and Mississippi. Here the relative minimum wage is especially important since RELMIN for all four states is above average and Mississippi registers the second highest value for the variable. Alabama and Tennessee also have unionization rates that are high for the south and about average values for EWMIX.

The relative minimum wage variable is also an important factor in explaining the case of New Mexico, which has very low wage flexibility in a region of high flexibility states. RELMIN for New Mexico is about one standard deviation above the mean for all states while the values for its neighbors, Texas, Arizona, Utah and Colorado, are at or slightly below the mean. In addition, New Mexico and Colorado are the two states in that group without a right-to-work law and New Mexico registers the lowest value for LAYOFF among the states. Low values of RELMIN help account for high wage flexibility in the Pacific Northwest. The value for RELMIN is more than one standard deviation below the mean for both Oregon and Washington, which has the second lowest value for this variable.

Two-Stage Estimates

It would appear easy to question the exogeneity of long-term unemployment and layoffs in the wage flexibility regressions reported above.

The link between wage flexibility and employment variability that is at the heart of much of recent macroeconomic theory would seem to argue that states with greater wage flexibility are likely to have fewer layoffs. And if wage rigidity causes fewer job vacancies in any given state of the economy, then there might be a negative relationship between wage flexibility and long-term unemployment. This section investigates this issue by specifying equations explaining both LTU and LAYOFF as a function of WFLEX and other variables and by estimating these regressions along with our model of the determinants of WFLEX by two-stage techniques.

While a detailed study of the determinants of long-term unemployment and layoff unemployment is beyond the scope of this chapter, we have identified a number of structural features of the state economy that are likely to be related to these variables (see Wunnava and Henley 1987). The exogenous control variables in the equation explaining LTU52 are: UNION; the average annual percentage change in real Gross State Product (GSP) from 1976 to 1986 (PCGSP); the average unemployment insurance replacement rate multiplied by the average fraction of the workforce insured over the 1964–1982 period (UI); and the average fraction of employment service applicants placed into jobs over the 1975–1980 period (ESPL). The exogenous variables in the equation explaining interstate differences in LAYOFF are: UNION, UI, the percentage of workers employed in manufacturing in 1973 (MFG), and the variance of the annual rate of real GSP growth over the 1976–1986 period. In addition to the exogenous variables in each equation, the list of instruments included dummy variables for three of the four major census regions of the country.

The two-stage generalized least squares (2SLS) estimates, weighting each variable as in the GLS regressions in table 3.2, are reported as equation (3.1) below. Standard errors are written in parentheses.

$$\text{WFLEX} = -5.68 - 42.40 \text{ EWMIX} + 10.58 \text{ SMALL} - 5.37 \text{ UNION}$$
$$\quad\;\; (6.25) \quad (5.62) \qquad\qquad (6.70) \qquad\qquad (2.10)$$

$$\qquad + .57 \text{ RTW} - 7.32 \text{ RELMIN} + 10.51 \text{ LAYOFF}$$
$$\qquad\quad (.20) \qquad\;\; (2.54) \qquad\qquad (2.58)$$

$$\qquad - 13.82 \text{ LTU52 } \bar{R}^2 = .88 \qquad\qquad\qquad\qquad (3.1)$$
$$\qquad\quad (9.87)$$

The two-stage estimates are similar to the GLS results reported in the previous section. The main effect of treating WFLEX, LAYOFF, and LTU52 as jointly endogenous variables is to raise substantially the coefficient estimate and significance level for LAYOFF and reduce slightly the estimated coefficients on SMALL, UNION, RTW, and RELMIN. Although the point estimate of the effect of LTU52 on WFLEX is increased here, so is the standard error of this variable. In general, the conclusions of the preceding section are not altered by the two-stage results.

The 2SLS coefficients for the long-term unemployment equation are (standard errors in parentheses):

$$LTU52 = .052 - .012 \ WFLEX + .074 \ UNION - .001 \ PCGSP$$
$$(.017) \ (.006) \qquad\quad (.030) \qquad\qquad (.018)$$

$$+ .084 \ UI - .008 \ ESPL \ \bar{R}^2 = .42 \qquad\qquad (3.2)$$
$$(.056) \quad\ (.004)$$

Wage flexibility has a statistically significant negative effect on long-term unemployment across the 48 states in this sample. This is consistent with the notion that wage flexibility enhances the efficiency of the search process in labor markets. Long-term unemployment is significantly higher in the most heavily unionized states, suggesting perhaps that workers prefer to queue for union jobs and accept a long duration of unemployment as the cost of doing so (Abowd and Farber 1982). Long-term unemployment is negatively related to the average annual rate of growth of real Gross State Product, although this coefficient estimate is substantially less than its standard error. All of the above-mentioned effects appear reasonable and the overall regression appears sound.

Regression (3.2) has some interesting results related to interstate differences in the unemployment insurance and employment service systems. The combined effect of more generous replacement rates and higher coverage acts to increase long-term unemployment, other things equal. This effect, however, is only marginally significant in the statistical sense. Greater public employment service effectiveness, as measured by the average placement rate, has a statistically significant negative relationship with long-term unemployment. Government action to improve the job search process through the activities of the public employment service can, thus, have an indirect effect on wage flexibility by reducing the fraction of the unemployed with long durations of unemployment.

Finally, the layoff unemployment regression results are:

$$\text{LAYOFF} = -.028 + .004 \text{ WFLEX} + .003 \text{ MFG} + .464 \text{ UI}$$
$$\qquad\qquad (.031) \ (.014) \qquad\quad (.0007) \qquad\ (.151)$$

$$\qquad + .127 \text{ UNION} + .008 \text{ VAR(PCGSP)} \ \bar{R}^2 = .50 \quad (3.3)$$
$$\qquad\ (.074) \qquad\qquad (.006)$$

Wage flexibility is found to have no relationship to the fraction of the unemployed on layoff. Union density has a positive and statistically significant effect in this equation as in that explaining LTU52. In addition to the direct effect of unionization on wage flexibility in equation (3.1), there are also important indirect effects of this variable in increasing both the duration of unemployment and the importance of layoffs as a cause of unemployment. The unemployment insurance variable has a positive effect on LAYOFF that is significant at the .05 level, suggesting that firms are more willing to use layoffs in states with more generous unemployment compensation systems. Like UNION, the unemployment insurance replacement rate appears to have a significant indirect effect on wage flexibility through its relationship with LTU52 and LAYOFF. Although we must interpret these coefficient estimates with caution, they do indicate that the unemployment insurance replacement rate may have a net positive effect on wage flexibility since the UI coefficient in the LAYOFF equation is about five times larger than that in the long-term unemployment regression and since LAYOFF is positively related to WFLEX. Finally, states with a more pronounced business cycle, as measured by the variance of annual real GSP growth rates and by the relative importance of manufacturing in the state economy, are also more likely to experience a greater degree of layoff unemployment.

Summary

The most widely accepted theoretical explanations for differences in aggregate wage flexibility across labor markets focus on factors that would cause firms within those labor markets to pay wages above the market-clearing rate and wages that are isolated from local unemployment. Differences between aggregate labor markets are then traced to differences in the proportions of firms in each area following nonmarket wage policies. One reason why firms may find it rational to pursue such wage policies is that they incorporate forecasts of appropriate wages into long-term contracts that cover periods which may have unemployment or inflation surprises. Or the firm may find that worker effort or efficiency is positively linked to the wage level making unjustified wage reductions counterproductive. Finally, wage setting in some firms may be closely linked to the bargaining power of insider workers who have little incentive to be responsive to the effect of their wage policy on the job prospects of unemployed workers who are outsiders to the firm.

This chapter attempted empirically to examine the ability of these wage rigidity theories to explain interstate differences in the responsiveness of wage inflation to unemployment. The results demonstrate considerable support for the efficiency wage and insider-outsider theories and for the hypothesis that union wage setting is a prominent factor leading to wage rigidity. We are able to draw four main conclusions about the determinants of interstate differences in wage flexibility:

(1) Wage flexibility is higher in states with a larger fraction of small enterprises and with an industry mix tilted away from those industries that Krueger and Summers (1988) identify as employing efficiency wage mechanisms. Both of these results provide at least an indirect test of the hypothesis that efficiency wages lead to wage rigidity. Our findings cannot reject that hypothesis.

(2) Wage flexibility is higher in states with relatively low rates of union membership and in states that have passed right-to-work laws. Both of these results are consistent with models tracing wage rigidity to the effects of collective bargaining contracts on the labor market.

(3) Wage flexibility is higher in states with a larger fraction of the

unemployed on layoff and in states with a smaller fraction of the unemployed with long durations of joblessness. These results are consistent with two insights from the insider-outsider model of wage determination: that insiders moderate wage demands when faced with the threat of insider job losses and that insiders do not consider the unemployment of outsiders in setting wages.

(4) Wage flexibility is higher in states where the statutory minimum wage relative to the average manufacturing wage is lower. It appears that minimum wages affect wage rigidity by limiting the extent to which average wages can be adjusted in a downward direction.

The basic results were found to hold for the most part even when long-term and layoff unemployment were treated as jointly endogenous variables with WFLEX. The two-stage results uncovered a strong, simultaneous relationship between wage flexibility and the fraction of the unemployed out of work for more than a year. Long-term unemployment was found to have a strong negative effect on wage flexibility, and wage flexibility was negatively related to long-term unemployment across the 48 states. While the two-stage results suggested a stronger effect of layoff unemployment on wage flexibility than did the OLS estimates, there was no evidence that wage flexibility was a significant determinant of interstate differences in layoffs as a cause of unemployment.

The two-stage results also suggested important indirect effects of union density, unemployment insurance benefits, and public employment service effectiveness on wage flexibility. Union density is seen as affecting wage flexibility differences across the 48 states indirectly by increasing both long-term and layoff unemployment. The variable measuring the combined effects of the unemployment insurance replacement and worker coverage rates was also positively related to both long-term unemployment and layoff unemployment. And the effectiveness of the public employment service, as measured by the average fraction of applicants placed in jobs, had a statistically significant negative relationship with long-term unemployment. Neither of these variables had a statistically significant effect when added directly to the wage flexibility regressions.

4

Conclusion

The purpose of this project has been to attempt to provide additional empirical information about the dynamics of regional labor markets that could also provide some insight into the important theoretical problem of wage rigidity. In doing so, we feel we have made two important contributions. First, we have specified a relatively simple labor market model that treats wage inflation and unemployment as jointly endogenous variables and that fits the data well for most of the states and metropolitan areas studied over the 1964–1986 period. Our second contribution has been a successful effort to test, at least indirectly, hypotheses about the determinants of wage rigidity contained in recent theoretical contributions. This summary of our findings first reviews the empirical results regarding wage inflation, unemployment and the determinants of wage rigidity before turning to a brief discussion of the policy implications of our study.

Regional Wage Inflation

Our analysis of wage inflation starts with a rudimentary Phillips curve model that treats regional wage inflation as a function of regional unemployment and national price inflation lagged one year. Despite its simplicity, the model does quite well in fitting the time series data for most of the states. Regressions of actual wage inflation on the rate of wage inflation forecast by the model for the 1964–86 period yield R^2 statistics greater than .65 for 33 of the 48 states. In addition, the coefficient estimates are generally statistically significant and of reasonable magnitudes.

One issue that has received some attention in the past concerns whether or not wage inflation is transmitted from leading to lagging regions. Tests for spatial auto-correlation in our samples do not provide support for the existence of a regional inflation transmission hierarchy. Thus our approach of estimating the labor market model separately for each area appears justified, at least when, as here, annual data are used.

Of primary concern in the time series analysis is the estimated coefficient on the local unemployment rate in the Phillips curve regressions. This estimate of the slope of the Phillips relationship is our index of wage flexibility. We find that wage flexibility is lowest in the New England and Middle Atlantic states. In fact, the unemployment coefficients in the Phillips curve regressions for Maine, New Hampshire, Massachusetts, Connecticut, New York, New Jersey, and Delaware are not statistically different from zero using conventional significance levels. The only other state for which we reach the same conclusion is New Mexico. Estimated wage flexibility is highest for states west of the Mississippi, particularly for the Plains states, and for a few states in the Southeast. Our conclusion that wage flexibility varies systematically across the states is reinforced by our finding of regional clusters of states with similar flexibility estimates. It is reassuring to note that states with similar industry and population mixes, such as South and North Dakota or Ohio and Michigan, also have similar wage flexibility coefficients.

A number of recent empirical studies of wage inflation and unemployment in Europe have concluded that hysteresis in the process generating the equilibrium unemployment rate lowers the responsiveness of wages to the level of unemployment. We test for hysteresis in the state results by including lagged unemployment rates in the Phillips curves and examining the estimated effects of the level of unemployment and changes in unemployment on wage inflation. In general, our findings do not support the hysteresis hypothesis, although there is evidence of partial hysteresis in a number of states and hysteresis might explain the very slight response of wages to unemployment in some of the northeastern states.

Regional Unemployment

Our two-equation labor market model derives the unemployment equation, our Fisher curve, from an Okun's law relationship and a markup pricing equation. While the model treats unemployment as determined solely by demand forces and assumes constant the role of labor supply factors as explicit unemployment rate determinants, it nevertheless does an excellent job of fitting the time series on state unemployment rates. Regressions of actual unemployment on that fore-cast by our model for each state over the 1964–1986 time period generate R^2 statistics that are quite high in almost every case. In addition, the forecasts of unemployment rates over time for each state are also accurate in predicting the cross-state pattern of unemployment rates. The correlation coefficient across the 48 states between actual unemployment and that forecast by the time series model for each state was .939 for 1965 and .942 for 1985.

The success of the model in explaining unemployment changes over time as a response to demand influences contrasts with the results of Marston (1985) and Roback (1982), among others. These cross-section analyses of equilibrium unemployment rates in regional labor markets conclude that migration appears to offset quickly local demand shocks to employment and unemployment rates. However, studies by Topel (1986), Bartik (1991) and Holzer (1991) suggest that local demand shocks have fairly long-lasting effects on wages and unemployment, which seems to square with the results of the model. Still, a fruitful area of extension for our labor market model would be to incorporate labor force participation and net migration into the determination of unem-ployment rates.

The primary result from the labor market model is a fresh way of looking at two long-standing issues in labor economics. First, it allows us to view the scatter diagram of wage inflation and unemployment rates as the interaction of supply changes, through the Phillips curve, and demand changes, via the Fisher curve, rather than as evidence for or against the stability of the Phillips relationship. Second, it provides a new way of incorporating wage influences as a determinant of unem-ployment that contrasts in its statistical success with the attempts to discern the effect of real wage levels on cyclical movements in U.S. employment and unemployment.

We concentrate most of our attention on the results of applying the model to state data. Clearly, metropolitan areas are conceptually closer to our idea of a local labor market. However, problems of data availability and periodic changes in the boundaries of Metropolitan Statistical Areas (MSAs) limit the number of areas for which reasonably lengthy time series can be constructed. The results for 16 MSAs yield essentially the same conclusions about the geographic pattern of wage inflation and unemployment as do our results on state data.

Wage Flexibility

The substantial variation across the 48 states in our estimates of the responsiveness of wage inflation to unemployment allows us to test several hypotheses regarding the determinants of wage flexibility (or wage rigidity). While a few previous studies have generated evidence that wages are less responsive to unemployment in more unionized areas or industries, our examination extends to a test of hypotheses derived from the recently developed work in efficiency wage and insider-outsider bargaining theories. While our cross-section regressions test these hypotheses indirectly, they lead us to conclude that wages are less flexible in regional labor markets in which firms are more likely to use efficiency wage mechanisms, workers are more heavily unionized, and the structure of unemployment affects wage bargains in a manner consistent with the insider-outsider model.

We also find four ways in which policy measures seem to affect the responsiveness of wages to unemployment. Other things equal, wage flexibility was higher in the 19 states with right-to-work laws and in states with low relative minimum wages. We also found evidence of an indirect effect of the unemployment insurance replacement rate on wage flexibility operating through the effects of benefits on long-term unemployment and the relative importance of layoffs as a cause of unemployment. It is interesting that the net direction of this indirect effect of unemployment compensation on wage flexibility appears to be positive. This is because benefits increase the likelihood of layoffs as well as the duration of unemployment, and a high incidence of layoff unemployment is found to increase wage flexibility. Finally, the effectiveness of the public employment service, as measured by the average placement rate of applicants, also had an indirect effect on wage flexibility operating through the effects of the employment service placement rate on long-term unemployment. However, all of the results reported in chapter 3 should be regarded as preliminary and worthy of further investigation.

Policy Considerations

There are both macroeconomic and microeconomic policy issues related to this research.

On the macroeconomic side, our results are very much in line with the main policy conclusion of New-Keynesian economics (Gordon 1990a, p. 1163): ". . . the optimal objective of stabilization policy should be to stabilize the growth rate of nominal GNP." However, in addition to the numerous obstacles to achieving that objective through national economic policy, our research highlights the potential importance of regional factors in attempting to stabilize the growth of nominal Gross State Product (GSP) across many subnational jurisdictions.

While some variation in demand growth across the states is necessary to accommodate efficient geographic reallocations of resources and production, there may be a role for state-level fiscal policy or national regional policy to stabilize the growth rate of nominal GSP, relative to the growth of national aggregate demand. Simulations for 1982 and 1986 indicate that equalizing demand growth across the states would have had significant effects on the unemployment rates of individual states, but surprisingly little impact on the national average unemployment rate. Whether this finding reflects an unusual divergence in regional demand growth during the 1980s or is a more general phenomenon deserves further investigation.

While the effect of equalizing state demand growth on inflation really cannot be addressed by our model, we can speculate on one possible inflation effect. Our simulations show that the northeastern states would have had slower growth and higher unemployment in the economic recovery from 1982 to 1986 if local demand had grown at the national rate. Slower growth probably would have meant less real estate inflation and might have resulted in fewer real estate-related problems in the construction and banking industries in those states. An extension of our model to include housing market and product price effects appears highly warranted where the availability of data permits.

While it is possible to use the model to simulate the effects of stabilizing regional demand growth relative to national Gross National Product (GNP) growth, it is far more difficult to prescribe how this might come about in practice. Clearly, federal or state fiscal policy would have to be used for this target. However, there does not appear to be much political support for such policies at either level. The fact that a number of states facing budget problems in the 1991 recession were forced to consider spending cuts and tax increases, suggests that state fiscal policy may be destabilizing demand growth in certain regions. Still, further research into the potential for appropriately structured state fiscal policies to implement national efforts to stabilize GNP growth appears warranted (Bahl 1984).

The microeconomic policy considerations essentially involve two questions. Should the state or federal governments explicitly adopt increased wage flexibility as a policy objective? If so, how could government policy increase wage flexibility in regional labor markets?

The question of the desirability of wage flexibility receives no clear-cut answer from economic theory (Hahn and Solow 1986). Our results, however, suggest that there may be some beneficial effects from wage flexibility. Across the 48 states, wage flexibility is correlated with lower average wage inflation rates, albeit more variable wage inflation rates, over the business cycle. Wage flexibility is also correlated with lower average unemployment rates and less variation in joblessness over the cycle. And wage flexibility is correlated with a smaller incidence of long-duration joblessness across the states. Admittedly, these findings are by-products of our main line of inquiry in this study and the statistical evidence is not overwhelming. Still, there is some empirical evidence to suggest that unemployment problems may be less severe in areas with greater wage flexibility.

How to achieve wage flexibility also involves difficult questions, since our results suggest that wage flexibility reflects mainly the industry, size, and union mix of firms in the regional economy. The policy variables included in the analysis of the determinants of wage flexibility – whether or not the state has a right-to-work law and the relative minimum wage – are also structural variables that do not appear to lend themselves easily to marginal changes to accomplish a movement toward greater wage flexibility. This is especially true for right-to-work laws, since many observers regard the existence of such legislation to be a reflection of the citizens' pre-existing preferences regarding unions (Hirsch and Addison 1986). And a state's ranking with regard to the relative minimum wage depends more on its wage structure than on the statutory wage set by the federal government.

There are some state policies that might enhance regional wage flexibility as a side effect. To the extent that experiments to improve job search and retraining for displaced workers (Leigh 1989) succeed in lowering long-term unemployment, as is suggested by our result that a higher placement rate in the employment service lowers long-duration joblessness, this might have the added effect of increasing wage flexibility. Similarly, wage flexibility might be enhanced by a shift in economic development policy from traditional "smokestack chasing" to policies designed to encourage local entrepreneurship and small business development (Carroll, Hyde, and Hudson 1987). Indeed, our results could be taken to suggest that wage rigidity is a potential cost that must be weighed against the employment and tax benefits to be derived from traditional development policies designed to attract firms that are likely to use efficiency wage mechanisms.

Even in the absence of policies designed to increase wage flexibility, it is likely that wage flexibility will increase in the American economy in the near future. The ongoing transformation in the industrial, demographic and geographic composition of economic activity should, according to the analysis in chapter 3, result in more flexible wages. As these changes continue, the economy will, in a sense, provide an experiment to determine if greater wage flexibility does indeed improve labor market performance. An extension of this research to an examination of structural shifts in wage responsiveness would appear to be a worthwhile endeavor.

Appendix

Here we consider a number of issues related to the time series estimates of our labor market model reported in chapter 2. Since the main focus in that chapter is the measurement of the degree of wage flexibility in regional labor markets, it is necessary to consider whether those estimates are robust to changes in the method of estimation or the specification of variables. In general, we find that all of our estimates of α_1 are highly correlated across the states, indicating that those results are indeed robust and that we can consider the cross-section analysis in chapter 3 with a greater degree of confidence.

Differences in Estimation Method

In chapter 2 we reported coefficient estimates derived by the method of three-stage least squares (3SLS). The advantage of using 3SLS is that it is a full information method that generally has a smaller asymptotic variance-covariance matrix than single-equation estimators. The problem with 3SLS is that any misspecification in the system affects all the parameter estimates.

Hausman (1978) tests can be used to examine the exogeneity of regressors and thus to determine whether it is necessary to use more sophisticated estimators. The Hausman tests essentially examine whether or not the coefficients from alternative estimators are equal, taking into account differences in the variance-covariance matrices. In comparing ordinary least squares (OLS) with 2SLS estimates, the Hausman tests reject the null hypothesis of equality between the unemployment coefficients in the Phillips curves for 15 states at the 10 percent significance level and 8 states at the 5 percent level. Tests on the wage inflation coefficient in the Fisher curve reject equal estimates for 29 states at the 10 percent level and for 22 states at the 5 percent significance level. These results suggest that OLS may be an appropriate estimator for the Phillips curve except in a few cases, but question the exogeneity of wage inflation in OLS estimates of the Fisher curve. Hausman tests of the equality of coefficient estimates of the endogenous variables using 2SLS and 3SLS reject the null hypothesis at the 10 percent level for 24 states and at the 5 percent level for 19 states.

Table A.1 presents coefficient estimates using OLS, 2SLS and 3SLS for a select sample of states. The states included are the largest in each of the nine census regions. In the Phillips curve estimates, the main effect of using 2SLS or 3SLS appears to be to raise the estimate of α_1 in some cases. Across all 48 states, the α_1 estimates from the three methods are highly correlated. The correlation between the OLS and 2SLS estimates of α_1 across 48 states is .93 and that between the OLS and 3SLS estimates is .92. The correlation between the 2SLS and 3SLS estimates is .99. Clearly, our measure of regional differences in wage flexibility is not much affected by the method of estimation.

In the Fisher curve regressions reported in table A.1, the coefficient on wage inflation, β_3, is lower in the OLS regressions for all states, especially for Colorado. The indication is that β_3 may be biased toward zero in the OLS regressions. As further evidence for this bias, the unweighted mean of β_3 across all 48 states is .2456 in OLS regressions, .3540 in 2SLS regressions and .3674 in 3SLS regressions. There is also a difference in the correlation across all 48 states between the OLS, 2SLS and 3SLS results. The correlation coefficient for the OLS and 2SLS estimates of β_3 is .55 while the correlation coefficient between the 2SLS and 3SLS estimates of β_3 is .92.

Our conclusion from this examination of alternative estimators is that the method of estimation does not materially affect the calculated responsiveness of wage inflation to unemployment. All of the estimates of α_1 are highly correlated across the states. With regard to the Fisher curve, it appears that OLS may generate biased estimates of the response of wage inflation to unemployment and that an explicit treatment of the simultaneous relationship between the Phillips and Fisher curves

**Table A.1   A Comparison of OLS, 2SLS and 3SLS
Coefficient Estimates, Selected States, 1964–1986**

State		α_0	α_1	α_2	β_0	β_1	β_2	β_3
MA	OLS	4.07*	−.10	.52*	2.26*	.83*	−.40*	.34*
	2SLS	4.20*	−.14	.54*	1.93	.81*	−.41*	.42*
	3SLS	3.96*	−.12	.56*	1.52	.82*	−.40*	.46*
NY	OLS	3.64*	−.19	.70*	1.00	.84*	−.22*	.29*
	2SLS	3.74*	−.22	.72*	.53	.80*	−.21*	.38*
	3SLS	3.17*	−.09	.67*	.67	.77*	−.22*	.42*
IL	OLS	4.26*	−.56*	.99*	1.55*	.95*	−.37*	.27*
	2SLS	4.38*	−.59*	1.01*	1.11	.96*	−.38*	.34*
	3SLS	4.38*	−.58*	1.01*	.88	.97*	−.36*	.34*
MO	OLS	4.22*	−.46*	.84*	.61	.95*	−.26*	.31*
	2SLS	4.61*	−.60*	.90*	.45	.95*	−.28*	.34*
	3SLS	4.55*	−.59*	.90*	.34	.95*	−.26*	.34*
FL	OLS	4.29*	−.58*	.98*	2.58*	.74*	−.27*	.34*
	2SLS	5.18*	−.91*	1.17*	2.30*	.73*	−.28*	.43*
	3SLS	5.16*	−.91*	1.17*	2.20*	.73*	−.28*	.43*
TN	OLS	4.64*	−.40*	.84*	1.67*	.88*	−.32*	.34*
	2SLS	4.85*	−.47*	.88*	1.15	.88*	−.34*	.44*
	3SLS	4.79*	−.47*	.89*	.66	.90*	−.31*	.45*
TX	OLS	4.54*	−.75*	1.05*	1.18*	.87*	−.26*	.37*
	2SLS	5.69*	−1.01*	1.09*	1.13*	.88*	−.27*	.40*
	3SLS	5.71*	−1.01*	1.09*	1.14*	.87*	−.27*	.40*
CO	OLS	4.54*	−.84*	1.00*	1.34	.80*	−.08	.09
	2SLS	4.68*	−.88*	1.02*	1.69	.70*	−.26*	.46*
	3SLS	4.59*	−.85*	1.00*	.77	.77*	−.16*	.37*
CA	OLS	4.70*	−.62*	1.04*	2.01*	1.00*	−.39*	.30*
	2SLS	5.72*	−.81*	1.11*	1.87*	1.01*	−.41*	.34*
	3SLS	5.74*	−.82*	1.11*	1.89*	1.01*	−.41*	.34*

*=Significant at .05 level.

is called for. Given the Hausman tests discussed above and given that the
RESET statistics suggest few problems of specification error, we have
chosen to emphasize the 3SLS results in chapter 2.

The Effect of National Demand Growth

Our labor market model assumes that the growth of nominal Gross
State Product (GSP), our measure of regional demand growth, is exogenous. Our justification for this is that the two primary determinants
of GSP growth are national monetary policy and the demand in the rest
of the world for exports from the ith region. In order to check the
sensitivity of our estimates to this exogeneity assumption, we have
reestimated the model for each state using the growth in nominal Gross
National Product (GNP) for the country as a whole as an instrument for
state GSP growth.

The results for a nine-state subsample are reported in tables A.2 and
A.3. The Phillips curve estimates in table A.2 are very little affected —
the correlation across all 48 states in the estimates of α_1 between the
3SLS estimates with state GSP growth and national GNP growth is .98.
So again, the estimate of primary concern for this study is immaterially
affected by this change in the specification of the model.

The coefficient estimates for the Fisher curve reported in table A.3 do
change considerably, as might be expected. There is no clear pattern of
change evident in the results in table A.3. However, across all 48 states
there is a tendency for higher parameter values in Fisher curves estimated with national demand growth. For example, the mean value of β_2
across the 48 states is $-.2634$ using GSP growth and $-.3509$ in
regressions with GNP growth. Similarly, the mean estimate of β_3 is
.3674 in the GSP growth regressions and .4099 in those with GNP
growth.

Since the estimates of wage responsiveness to unemployment are
unaffected by this change in the model and since we believe it is possible
to regard state GSP growth as exogenously determined, we have decided
to use our original specification in the main body of this book.

Table A.2   Phillips Curve Estimates with National Demand Growth, Selected States, 1964–1986

State	α_0	α_1	α_2	R^2	d	RESET	Jarque-Bera
MA	4.18*	−.15	.56*	.66	1.37	2.40	5.15
NY	3.94*	−.28	.75*	.74	1.31	2.78	.40
IL	4.43*	−.61*	1.02*	.79	2.04	.25	.55
MO	4.44*	−.57*	.90*	.72	1.82	.89	11.66
FL	5.58*	−1.02*	1.23*	.74	1.13	3.53*	1.54
TN	4.86*	−.48*	.89*	.70	1.82	.41	2.28
TX	5.84*	−1.02*	1.08*	.88	1.87	.25	.54
CO	4.65*	−.87*	1.01*	.61	1.58	.46	1.14
CA	6.32*	−.92*	1.14*	.92	1.38	.44	1.09

Estimated using 3SLS. * = significant at .05 level. R^2 is that for an OLS regression of actual values on those forecast by the model.

Table A.3   Fisher Curve Estimates with National Demand Growth, Selected States, 1964–1986

State	β_0	β_1	β_2	β_3	R^2	h	RESET	Jarque-Bera
MA	−.43	.78*	−.18	.52*	.75	1.07	.08	3.36
NY	.20	.85*	−.22*	.46*	.87	2.14*	.21	2.20
IL	.63	1.02*	−.41*	.49*	.95	−1.08	.60	1.08
MO	.65	.89*	−.34*	.47*	.90	−.67	.20	1.15
FL	1.31	.89*	−.38*	.44*	.84	−.54	.04	3.93
TN	.60	.90*	−.47*	.63*	.92	−1.88	2.84	1.04
TX	1.42*	1.13*	−.34*	.18*	.86	−	.27	.61
CO	1.27	.89*	−.26*	.28*	.78	−	.47	.91
CA	2.47*	.88*	−.38*	.30*	.82	.21	.09	1.44

See footnotes to table A.2.

Statistical Problems

The array of tests in chapter 2 churned up a small number of potential problems in the statistical analysis of a few states. The present section is devoted to a consideration of those problems which appear when the diagnostic tests are applied at the 1 percent significance level. Particular attention will be paid to the question of whether or not the statistical hiccoughs identified here bias the estimate of the unemployment coefficient in the Phillips curve.

Attention in this section will first be concentrated upon just five states: Missouri, Washington, Colorado, Idaho, and Wyoming. The Phillips curve for Missouri in table 2.1 violates the assumption of normally distributed residuals. The Phillips curve for Washington in table 2.1 violates the assumption of serially independent residuals. The Fisher curve for Colorado in table 2.2 violates the same assumption. The Fisher curves for Idaho and Wyoming, also reported in Table 2.2, are, according to the RESET test, misspecified.

The problemsolving approach adopted in this section is as follows. Where residuals are non-normally distributed, we identify any obvious outliers and introduce a dichotomous variable into the relevant equation for each of the outlying periods; each of these variables takes unit value for the outlying period, and is zero in all other periods. Where residuals are serially correlated, the 3SLS is repeated, using the Cochrane-Orcutt transformations of the original variables. Finally, where the RESET indicates the possible presence of misspecification, we introduce into the right-hand side of an equation a quadratic term in the lagged dependent variable. The results obtained by applying these methods are reported in table A.4 (Phillips curves) and table A.5 (Fisher curves).

In the case of Missouri, examination of the Phillips curve regression residuals indicates the presence of an outlying observation in 1977. In that year, observed wage inflation was substantially higher than predicted by the model. Including a 1977 dummy in the Phillips curve (and as an instrumental variable) considerably improves the results obtained for this state. The coefficient of greatest interest in the present study — the unemployment coefficient in the Phillips curve — is virtually un-

Table A.4 Phillips Curve Estimates, Corrected for Statistical Problems, 5 States, 1964–1986

$$W = \alpha_0 + \alpha_1 U + \alpha_2 P_{-1} + \alpha_3 D72 + \alpha_4 D73 + \alpha_5 D77$$

State	Cochrane-Orcutt	α_0	α_1	α_2	α_3	α_4	α_5	R^2	d	RESET	Jarque-Bera
MO	no	4.3420	−.5599	.8763			4.5361	.867	2.05	.153	1.204
		(.5532)	(.1272)	(.0899)			(.9065)				
WA	yes	3.7957	−1.2220	1.2078				.697	1.81	1.186	1.296
		(1.0116)	(.32251)	(.1991)							
CO	yes	6.5150	−.9496	1.0843				.679	1.13	.373	.928
		(1.6545)	(.3092)	(.1728)							
ID	no	7.2922	−.8698	.8112				.279	2.49	.747	.990
		(2.0515)	(.3806)	(.2217)							
WY	no	2.5593	−.3846	.9357	−9.1866	10.8802		.753	2.31	.078	.236
		(1.9403)	(.3206)	(.1586)	(2.0466)	(2.1174)					

Standard errors in parentheses. The terms D72, D73 and D77 refer to dummy variables which each take zero value for all years but one; the exceptions are, respectively, 1972, 1973 and 1977. In the case of the Cochrane-Orcutt 3SLS regressions, the time period covered is 1966–1986.

Table A.5   Fisher Curve Estimates, Corrected for Statistical Problems, 5 States, 1964–1986

$$U = \beta_0 + \beta_1 U_{-1} + \beta_2 y + \beta_3 W + \beta_4 U^2_{-1}$$

State	Cochrane-Orcutt	β_0	β_1	β_2	β_3	β_4	R^2	h	RESET	Jarque-Bera
MO	no	.4251	.9545	−.2784	.3499		.884	−1.63	.683	.911
		(.6440)	(.0808)	(.0574)	(.0757)					
WA	yes	2.3113	.4844	−.1932	.0746		.507	−2.43	.446	1.054
		(.6535)	(.1457)	(.0555)	(.1191)					
CO	yes	2.2227	.7430	−.1616	.2539		.855	—	.237	1.007
		(.9759)	(.1041)	(.0549)	(.0735)					
ID	no	−4.7634	2.4758	−.1007	.2122	−.1135	.850	—	1.649	.443
		(3.2944)	(1.1376)	(.0750)	(.2002)	(.0833)				
WY	no	2.3677	.5911	−.0741	.0638		.716	—	1.902	1.351
		(1.0942)	(.1929)	(.0278)	(.0572)					

Standard errors in parentheses. In the case of the Cochrane–Orcutt 3SLS regressions, the time period covered is 1966–1986.

changed as a result of this improvement in the specification of the model. Changes in the other estimated coefficients are also minimal.

The problem of auto-correlation in the residuals of the Phillips curve for Washington may be checked by applying 3SLS to the Cochrane-Orcutt transformed variables. This procedure has a slight impact upon the unemployment coefficient in the Phillips curve, raising it a little above the value observed in table 2.1. Correcting for auto-correlated residuals in this manner reduces the coefficient on expected price inflation in the Phillips curve, which now becomes insignificantly different from unity. In the Fisher curve, the unemployment persistence coefficient is reduced when the Cochrane-Orcutt transformations are applied.

Correction of the serial correlation observed in the Fisher curve residuals in Colorado also has a rather slight effect on the unemployment coefficient of the Phillips curve. The coefficient again rises somewhat in absolute terms, indicating that wages in that state are rather more responsive to external labor market conditions than the basic model (uncorrected for serial correlation) would imply.

The inclusion on the right-hand side of the Fisher curve of a lagged and squared dependent variable succeeds in eliminating the misspecification bias observed in Idaho. The impact of this specification change upon the Phillips curve is slight. In the Fisher curve, the coefficients on aggregate demand growth and wage inflation both still fall a little short of significance at the conventional levels. The latter coefficient implies a slightly higher Okun coefficient than was the case in the basic model. Inevitably, though, the greatest impact is on the lagged unemployment rate coefficient; an unfortunate cost of the correction of misspecification bias is that we can no longer interpret this term as a measure of persistence.

The case of Wyoming is somewhat unusual. The main source of concern is the high RESET value obtained in the Fisher curve, but there is evidence of problems other than functional misspecification. In particular, the within-sample forecasting power of the Phillips curve is weak, and an examination of the residuals generated by this latter function indicates that there may be substantial measurement error in the dependent variable in 1972. At this time there was a revision of the

Standard Industrial Classification; the consequent redefinition of the manufacturing sector results in a break in the state-specific wage series at this time. While a number of states were likely affected by this change, the impact was nowhere as severe as in Wyoming – this is the only state to have measured a decrease in wages between 1971 and 1972. To correct for this, we insert dummy variables for 1972 and 1973 into the Phillips curve equation. This has two main effects. First, the diagnostics indicate substantially improved performance of the model. In particular, the RESET statistic associated with the Fisher curve falls dramatically to 1.90. Second, the unemployment coefficient in the Phillips curve is closer to zero than is the case in the uncorrected model; this indicates that wages are relatively less flexible to local labor market conditions.

In this section, we have tackled head-on the small number of statistical problems churned up by the implementation of the basic model to state-specific data. It has been essential to fix up these problems at this stage; misspecification of the model and non-normal residual terms can both lead to biased estimates, while the presence of auto-correlated residuals implies that the predictions of the model are inefficient. Fortunately, as we have seen, it turns out that the estimates of wage flexibility provided by the basic model of the last section are changed but little when we correct for the various statistical problems encountered.

We now turn to fixing up the problems identified by the diagnostic tests for metropolitan areas. We therefore concentrate on just five metropolitan areas: Boston, Dallas-Fort Worth, Washington DC, Detroit, and Minneapolis-St. Paul. The Phillips and Fisher curves, corrected for the statistical problems identified above, are reported respectively in tables A.6 and A.7.

The misspecification in the Phillips curve obtained for Boston in the basic model can be checked by introducing a quadratic term in the lagged dependent variable. This leaves most of the regression coefficients virtually unchanged. The exception, predictably enough, is the expected price inflation term in the Phillips curve; the specification change renders the interpretation of this coefficient unclear. It would appear, however, that the inclusion of the new term in the Phillips curve

Table A.6 Phillips Curve Estimates, Corrected for Statistical Problems,
5 SMSAs, 1964–1986

$$w = \alpha_0 + \alpha_1 U + \alpha_{2P-1} + \alpha_3 D78 + \alpha_4 D84 + \alpha_5 w^2_{-1}$$

	Cochrane-Orcutt	α_0	α_1	α_2	α_3	α_4	α_5	R^2	d	RESET	Jarque-Bera
Boston	no	3.7410	.0536	.2160			.0284	.608	1.91	4.016	.699
		(.5457)	(.1277)	(.1075)			(.0141)				
Dallas–Ft. Worth	no	5.1972	−.8171	.9494		−6.7318		.814	2.22	.286	.563
		(1.0520)	(.2979)	(.1162)		(1.3560)					
Washington, DC	no	9.1056	−2.8404	1.4346	16.4590			.547	1.26	.156	.273
		(3.3703)	(1.1584)	(.6333)	(3.4216)						
Detroit	yes	7.9970	−.4825	1.0388				.649	1.31	.225	1.360
		(1.3866)	(.1447)	(.2031)							
Minneapolis–St. Paul	yes	4.4063	−.3577	.8957				.727	.73	1.903	.732
		(1.2457)	(.2428)	(.1374)							

Table A.7 Fisher Curve Estimates, Corrected for Statistical Problems, 5 SMSAs, 1964–1986

$$U = \beta_0 + \beta_1 U_{-1} + \beta_2 y + \beta_3 w$$

	Cochrane-Orcutt	β_0	β_1	β_2	β_3	R^2	h	RESET	Jarque-Bera
Boston	no	.3453 (1.2997)	.7604 (.1140)	−.3636 (.0933)	.6433 (.1981)	.862	.81	.115	1.11
Dallas–Ft. Worth	no	1.2233 (.8191)	.7015 (.1642)	−.1412 (.0440)	.2240 (.0722)	.709	−.12	.132	1.951
Washington, DC	no	1.3503 (.9228)	.8392 (.1126)	−.1013 (.0989)	.0508 (.0355)	.764	−2.00	.143	2.202
Detroit	yes	3.6580 (.9378)	.8931 (.0493)	−.4032 (.0419)	.2320 (.0804)	.948	—	.681	.650
Minneapolis–St. Paul	yes	2.7788 (.6487)	.6312 (.0815)	−.2764 (.0440)	.3171 (.0579)	.890	—	1.354	1.307

satisfactorily proxies the missing variable, since the RESET statistic falls dramatically as a result.

The observed non-normality of residuals in the Phillips curve for Washington can be removed by inserting into the Phillips curve a dichotomous variable which takes unit value for 1978 and is zero in all other years. This has a number of beneficial effects. First, the Jarque-Bera statistic for the Phillips curve falls back into line, indicating that the source of non-Gaussian residuals has been removed. Second, the determination coefficient associated with the Phillips curve improves considerably. Third, the RESET statistic for the Fisher curve falls sharply, suggesting that this function is now correctly specified. It should be noted, however, that the coefficient on wage inflation obtained in the Fisher curve is still low in relation to its hypothesized value. Re-running the system, this time including a 1978 dummy also in the Fisher curve equation, raises this coefficient to 0.25 (with a t ratio of 3.05), and has little effect on the other coefficients and most of the diagnostics; we do not report in full the result of this regression, however, since there is evidence that the Fisher curve is misspecified—the RESET statistic is 5.01. It is clear that 1978 was not a typical year in Washington.

The presence of non-normal residuals in the Phillips curve for Dallas can also be checked by the inclusion in the Phillips function of a dummy variable. This time the non-normality is due to an outlying observation in 1984, which reduces wage inflation below its expected value. The estimated parameters of the model are not, in this instance, greatly affected by the inclusion of the dummy variable.

To correct for serial correlation in the Fisher curves obtained for Detroit and Minneapolis-St. Paul we have used 3SLS on the Cochrane-Orcutt transformed variables. The impact upon the coefficient estimates is slight in both instances.

References

Abowd, J.M. and H.S. Farber. 1982. "Job Queues and the Union Status of Workers," *Industrial and Labor Relations Review* 35: 354-67.

Akerlof, G.A. and J.L. Yellen. 1990. "The Fair Wage-Effort Hypothesis and Unemployment," *Quarterly Journal of Economics* 105: 255-84.

Azariadis, C. 1975. "Implicit Contracts and Underemployment Equilibria," *Journal of Political Economy* 83: 1183-1202.

Bahl, R. 1984. "The Growing Fiscal and Economic Importance of State and Local Governments." In *Financing State and Local Governments in the 1980s*. New York: Oxford University Press.

Baily, M. 1974. "Wages and Employment Under Uncertain Demand," *Review of Economic Studies* 41: 37-50.

Barro, R.J. 1988. "The Persistence of Unemployment," *American Economic Review, Papers and Proceedings* 78: 32-37.

Barro, R.J. 1989. "An Efficiency-Wage Theory of the Weather," *Journal of Political Economy* 97: 999-1001.

Bartik, T.J. 1991. *Who Benefits From State and Local Economic Development Policies?* Kalamazoo, MI: W.E. Upjohn Institute for Employment Research.

Beare, J.B. 1976. "A Monetarist Model of Regional Business Cycles," *Journal of Regional Science* 16: 57-63.

Blackaby, D.H. and D.N. Manning. 1990. "Earnings, Unemployment and the Regional Employment Structure in Britain," *Regional Studies* 24: 529-535.

Blackley, P.R. 1989. "The Measurement and Determination of State Equilibrium Unemployment Rates," *Southern Economic Journal* 56: 440-456.

Blanchard, O.J. and L.H. Summers. 1987. "Hysteresis in Unemployment," *European Economic Review* 31: 288–295.

———. 1988. "Hysteresis and the European Unemployment Problem." In *Unemployment, Hysteresis and the Natural Rate Hypothesis*, ed. R. Cross. Oxford: Blackwell.

Blanchard, O.J. and S. Fischer. 1989. *Lectures on Macroeconomics*. Cambridge: MIT Press.

Blanchflower, D.G. and A.J. Oswald. 1990. "The Wage Curve," *Scandinavian Journal of Economics* 92: 215–235.

Blinder, A.S. and D.H. Choi. 1990. "A Shred of Evidence on Theories of Wage Stickiness," *Quarterly Journal of Economics* 105: 1003–1015.

Brown, C. 1988. "Minimum Wage Laws: Are They Overrated?" *Journal of Economic Perspectives* 2: 133–145.

———. 1990. "Firms' Choice of Method of Pay," *Industrial and Labor Relations Review* 43: 165–182.

Bruno, M. and J. Sachs. 1985. *The Economics of Worldwide Stagflation*. Cambridge: Harvard University Press.

Bureau of National Affairs. 1983. *Basic Patterns in Union Contracts*, 10th ed. Washington, DC: Bureau of National Affairs.

Burtless, G. 1987. "Jobless Pay and High European Unemployment," In *Barriers to European Growth*, ed. R.Z. Lawrence and C.L. Schultze. Washington, DC: Brookings.

Card, D. 1990. "Unexpected Inflation, Real Wages, and Employment Determination in Union Contracts," *American Economic Review* 80: 669–88.

Carmichael, H.L. 1990. "Efficiency Wage Models of Unemployment — One View," *Economic Inquiry* 28: 269–295.

Carroll, J.J., M.S. Hyde, and W.E. Hudson. 1987. "State-Level Perspectives on Industrial Policy," *Economic Development Quarterly* 1: 333–342.

Carruth, A.A. and A.J. Oswald. 1987. "Wage Inflexibility in Britain," *Oxford Bulletin of Economics and Statistics* 49: 59–78.

Chan-Lee, J.H., D.T. Coe, and M. Prywes. 1987. "Microeconomic

Changes and Macroeconomic Wage Disinflation in the 1980s," *OECD Economic Studies* 8: 121–55.

Clark, A. 1990. "Efficient Bargains and the McDonald-Solow Conjecture," *Journal of Labor Economics* 8: 502–28.

Clark, G.L. 1981. "The Regional Impact of Stagflation: A Conceptual Model and Empirical Evidence for Canada." In *Regional Wage Inflation and Unemployment*, ed. R.L. Martin. London: Pion.

Clark, G.L., M.S. Gertler, and J. Whiteman. 1986. *Regional Dynamics: Studies in Adjustment Theory*. Boston: Unwin Hyman.

Coe, D.T. 1985. "Nominal Wages, the NAIRU and Wage Flexibility," *OECD Economic Studies* 5: 87–126.

———. 1988. "Hysteresis Effects in Aggregate Wage Equations." In *Unemployment, Hysteresis and the Natural Rate Hypothesis*, ed. R.B. Cross. Oxford: Blackwell.

Davidson, C. 1990. *Recent Developments in the Theory of Involuntary Unemployment*. Kalamazoo, MI: W.E. Upjohn Institute for Employment Research.

Doeringer, P. and M. Piore 1971. *Internal Labor Markets and Manpower Analysis*. Lexington, MA: Heath.

Ehrenberg, R.G. and R.L. Oaxaca. 1976. "Unemployment Insurance, Duration of Unemployment and Subsequent Wage Gain," *American Economic Review* 66: 754–86.

Ehrenberg, R.G. and R.S. Smith. 1991. *Modern Labor Economics*, 4th ed. New York: HarperCollins.

Fisher, I. 1926. "A Statistical Relation Between Unemployment and Price Changes," *International Labor Review* 13: 317–323 (reprinted in *Journal of Political Economy* 81: 496–502).

Flanagan, R.J. 1984. "Wage Concessions and Long-Term Union Wage Flexibility," *Brookings Papers on Economic Activity* 1: 183–216.

Franz, W. 1987. "Hysteresis, Persistence and the NAIRU: an Empirical Analysis for the FRG." In *The Fight Against Unemployment*, ed. P.R.G. Layard and L. Calmfors. Cambridge: MIT Press.

Friedman, M. 1968. "The Role of Monetary Policy," *American Economic Review* 48: 1–17.

————. 1976. *Price Theory*. Chicago: Aldine.

Gordon, R.J. 1990a. "What is New-Keynesian Economics?" *Journal of Economic Literature* 28: 1115–1171.

————. 1990b. *Macroeconomics*, 5th ed. Glenview, IL: Scott, Foresman.

Granger, C.W.J., R. Engle, R. Ramanathan, and A. Andersen. 1979. "Residential Load Curves and Time-of-Day Pricing: An Econometric Analysis," *Journal of Econometrics* 9: 13–32.

Groshen, E.L. 1988. "Sources of Wage Dispersion: The Contribution of Inter-employer Wage Differentials Within Industry," Federal Reserve Bank of Cleveland Working Paper 8802.

Grossman, S. and O. Hart. 1981. "Implicit Contracts, Moral Hazard, and Unemployment," *American Economic Review* 71: 301–307.

Grubb, D. 1986. "Topics in the OECD Phillips Curve," *Economic Journal* 96: 55–79.

Grubb, D., R. Jackman, and R. Layard. 1983. "Wage Rigidity and Unemployment in OECD Countries," *European Economic Review* 21: 11–39.

Hahn, F.H. and R.M. Solow. 1986. "Is Wage Flexibility a Good Thing?" In *Wage Rigidity and Unemployment*, ed. W. Beckerman. Baltimore: The Johns Hopkins Press.

Hall, R.E. 1975. "The Rigidity of Wages and the Persistence of Unemployment," *Brookings Papers on Economic Activity* 6: 301–335.

Hargreaves-Heap, S.P. 1980. "Choosing the Wrong Natural Rate: Accelerating Inflation or Decelerating Employment and Growth?" *Economic Journal* 90: 611–620.

Hausman, J.A. 1978. "Specification Tests in Econometrics," *Econometrica* 46: 1251–71.

Helliwell, J.F. 1988. "Comparative Macroeconomics of Stagflation," *Journal of Economic Literature* 26: 1–28.

Hirsch, B.T. and J.T. Addison. 1986. *The Economic Analysis of Unions*. Boston: Allen & Unwin.

Holzer, H. 1991. "Employment, Unemployment and Demand Shifts in Local Labor Markets," *Review of Economics and Statistics* 73: 25–32.

Hudson, J.R. 1988. *Unemployment after Keynes*. New York: Harvester-Wheatsheaf.

Hyclak, T.J. and G. Johnes. 1989. "Real Wage Rigidity in Regional Labor Markets in the UK, the US and West Germany," *Journal of Regional Science* 29: 423–432.

———. 1990. "Wage Inflation and Unemployment Dynamics in the UK and US: a Longer View," Martindale Center Discussion Paper, 1990 Series – No. 6, Lehigh University.

———. 1992. "Regional Wage Inflation and Unemployment Dynamics in Great Britain," *Scottish Journal of Political Economy*, forthcoming.

Jackman, R., R. Layard and S. Savouri. 1990. "Labour-Market Mismatch: A Framework for Thought," Centre for Economic Performance, Discussion Paper No. 1, London School of Economics.

Jarque, C.M. and A.K. Bera. 1980. "Efficient Tests for Normality, Homoscedasticity, and Serial Independence of Regression Residuals," *Economics Letters* 6: 255–259.

Johnes, G. and T.J. Hyclak. 1989. "Wage Inflation and Unemployment in Europe: the Regional Dimension," *Regional Studies* 23: 19–24.

Johnson, G.E. and P.R.G. Layard. 1986. "The Natural Rate of Unemployment: Explanation and Policy." In *Handbook of labor economics*, ed. O. Ashenfelter and P.R.G. Layard. Amsterdam: North Holland.

Johnson, T.R., K.P. Dickinson and R.W. West. 1985. "An Evaluation of the Impact of Employment Service Referrals on Applicant Earnings," *Journal of Human Resources*, 20: 117–137.

Katz, A. 1977. "Contributions of the Employment Service to Applicant Earnings," *Labor Law Journal* 28: 472–478.

Katz, L. 1986. "Efficiency Wage Theories: A Partial Evaluation." In *NBER Macroeconomics Annual 1986*, ed. S. Fischer. Cambridge: MIT Press.

Kaun, D.E. and M.H. Spiro. 1970. "The Relation Between Wages and Unemployment in U.S. Cities 1955–1965," *The Manchester School of Economics and Social Studies* 38: 1–14.

Keynes, J.M. 1936. *The General Theory of Employment, Interest and Money*. London: Macmillan.

Klau, F. and A. Mittelstadt. 1986. "Labor Market Flexibility," *OECD Economic Studies* 6: 7–45.

Kniesner, T.J. and A.H. Goldsmith. 1987. "A Survey of Alternative Models of the Aggregate U.S. Labor Market," *Journal of Economic Literature* 25: 1241–1280.

Krueger, A.B. and L.H. Summers. 1987. "Reflections on the Inter-Industry Wage Structure." In *Unemployment and the Structure of Labor Markets*, ed. K. Lang and J.S. Leonard. New York: Basil Blackwell.

———. 1988. "Efficiency Wages and the Inter-industry Wage Structure," *Econometrica* 56: 259–293.

Lampe, D.R. (ed.). 1988. *The Massachusetts Miracle*. Cambridge: MIT Press.

Lang, K. and S. Kahn. 1990. "Efficiency Wage Models of Unemployment: A Second View," *Economic Inquiry* 28: 296–306.

Layard, P.R.G. and C.R. Bean. 1989. "Why Does Unemployment Persist?" *Scandinavian Journal of Economics* 91: 371–396.

Layard, P.R.G. and S.J. Nickell. 1986. "Unemployment in Britain," In *The Rise in Unemployment*, ed. C.R. Bean, P.R.G. Layard and S.J. Nickell. Oxford: Blackwell.

Layard, P.R.G., S. Nickell and R. Jackman. 1991. *Unemployment: Macroeconomic Performance and the Labour Market*. Oxford: Oxford University Press.

Lazear, E.P. 1981. "Agency, Earnings Profiles, Productivity and Hours Restrictions," *American Economic Review* 71: 606–620.

Leigh, D.E. 1989. *Assisting Displaced Workers: Do the States Have a Better Idea?* Kalamazoo, MI: W.E. Upjohn Institute for Employment Research.

Lesage, J.P. and J.D. Reed. 1989. "Interregional Wage Transmission in an Urban Hierarchy: Tests Using Vector Autoregressive Models," *International Regional Science Review* 12: 305–318.

———. 1990. "Testing Criteria for Determining Leading Regions in Wage Transmission Models," *Journal of Regional Science* 30: 37–50.

Lindbeck, A. and D. Snower. 1988. *The Insider-Outsider Theory of Employment and Unemployment*. Cambridge: MIT Press.

Lucas, R.E. 1972. "Expectations and the Neutrality of Money," *Journal of Economic Theory* 4: 103–124.

———. 1973. "Some International Evidence on Output-Inflation Trade-offs," *American Economic Review* 63: 326–334.

———. 1978. "Unemployment Policy," *American Economic Review, Papers and Proceedings* 68: 353–357.

Mackay, D.I. and R.A. Hart. 1975. "Wage Inflation and the Regional Wage Structure." In *Contemporary Issues in Economics*, ed. M. Parkin and R. Nobay. Manchester: Manchester University Press.

Markusen, A. 1985. *Profit Cycles, Oligopoly and Regional Development*. Cambridge: MIT Press.

Marston, S. 1985. "Two Views of the Geographic Distribution of Unemployment," *Quarterly Journal of Economics* 100: 57–59.

Martin, R.L. 1981. "Wage Change Interdependence Amongst Regional Labour Markets: Conceptual Issues and Some Empirical Evidence for the United States." In *Regional Wage Inflation and Unemployment*, ed. R.L. Martin. London: Pion.

Mathur, V.K. 1976. "The Relation Between Rate of Change of Money Wage Rates and Unemployment in Local Labor Markets: Some New Evidence," *Journal of Regional Science* 16: 389–398.

McDonald, I.M. and R.M. Solow. 1981. "Wage Bargaining and Employment," *American Economic Review* 71: 896–908.

Minford, A.P.L., P. Ashton, M. Peel, D. Davies and A. Sprague. 1985. *Unemployment: Cause and Cure*. Blackwell: Oxford.

Mitchell, D.J.B. 1980. *Unions, Wages, and Inflation*. Washington, DC: The Brookings Institution.

Moore, W.J. and R.J. Newman. 1985. "The Effects of Right to Work Laws: A Review of the Literature," *Industrial and Labor Relations Review* 38: 571–85.

Nickell, S.J. 1987. "Why is Wage Inflation in Britain So High?" *Oxford Bulletin of Economics and Statistics* 49: 103–128.

———. 1990. "Unemployment: A Survey," *Economic Journal* 100: 391–439.

Okun, A.M. 1962. "Potential GNP: Its Measurement and Significance," *Proceedings of the Business and Economic Statistics Section of the*

American Statistical Association, Washington DC, 98–103; reprinted in Pechman, J.A. (ed.) (1983) *Economics for policy-making: selected essays of Arthur M. Okun*. Cambridge: MIT Press.

———. 1981. *Prices and Quantities: A Macroeconomic Analysis*. Washington, DC: Brookings Institution.

Phelps, E. 1967. "Phillips Curves, Expectations of Inflation and Optimal Unemployment Over Time," *Economica* 34: 254–281.

Phillips, A.W. 1958. "The Relation Between Unemployment and the Rate of Change of Money Wage Rates in the United Kingdom, 1861–1957," *Economica* 25: 283–299.

Pierre, A.J. (ed.) 1984. *Unemployment and Growth in the Western Economies*. New York: Council on Foreign Relations.

Pigou, A.C. 1913. *Unemployment*. London: Williams and Norgate.

Ramsey, J.B. 1969. "Tests for Specification Errors in Classical Linear Least Squares Regression Analysis," *Journal of the Royal Statistical Society* 31: Series B, 350–371.

Roback, J. 1982. "Wages, Rents and the Quality of Life," *Journal of Political Economy* 90: 1257–1277.

Rodwin, L. and H. Sazanami (eds.). 1989. *Deindustrialization and Regional Economic Transformation*. Boston: Unwin Hyman.

Salop, S. 1979. "A Model of the Natural Rate of Unemployment," *American Economic Review* 69: 117–125.

Sargent, T.J. 1973. "Rational Expectations, the Real Rate of Interest, and the Natural Rate of Unemployment," *Brookings Papers on Economic Activity* 4: 429–472.

Sargent, T.J. and Wallace, N. 1975. "Rational Expectations, the Optimal Monetary Instrument and the Optimal Money Supply Rule," *Journal of Political Economy* 83: 241–254.

Schultze, C.L. 1985. "Microeconomic Efficiency and Nominal Wage Stickiness," *American Economic Review* 75: 1–15.

Smith, S.K. and Ahmed, B. 1990. "A Demographic Analysis of the Population Growth of States, 1950–1980," *Journal of Regional Science* 30: 209–227.

Summers, L.H. 1988. "Relative Wages, Efficiency Wages and Keynesian Unemployment," *American Economic Review, Papers and Proceedings* 78: 383–388.

Taylor, J.B. 1979. "Staggered Wage Setting in a Macro Model," *American Economic Review* 69: 108–113.

Thirlwall, A.P. 1969. "Demand Disequilibrium in the Labor Market and Wage Rate Inflation in the United Kingdom," *Yorkshire Bulletin of Economic and Social Research* 21: 66–76.

———. 1970. "Regional Phillips Curves," *Bulletin of the Oxford Institute of Economics and Statistics* 32: 19–32.

Tiebout, C.M. 1956. "A Pure Theory of Local Expenditures," *Journal of Political Economy* 64: 416–424.

Topel, R.H. 1983. "On Layoffs and Unemployment Insurance," *American Economic Review* 73: 541–59.

———. 1986. "Local Labor Markets," *Journal of Political Economy* 94: S111–S143.

Troy, L. and Sheflin, N. 1985. *Union Sourcebook*. West Orange, NJ: IRDIS.

Turnovsky, S.J. and M.L. Wachter. 1972. "A Test of the Expectations Hypothesis Using Directly Observed Wage and Price Expectations," *Review of Economics and Statistics* 54: 47–54.

Wachter, M.L. and W.H. Carter. 1989. "Norm Shifts in Union Wages: Will 1989 Be a Replay of 1969?" *Brookings Papers on Economic Activity* 2: 233–271.

Wadsworth, J. 1991. "Unemployment Benefits and Search Efforts in the UK Labour Market," *Economica* 58: 17–34.

White, H. 1980. "A Heteroskedasticity-Consistent Covariance Matrix Estimator and Direct Test for Heteroskedasticity," *Econometrica* 48: 817–38.

Wulwick, N.J. 1987. "The Phillips Curve: Which? Whose? To Do What? How?" *Southern Economic Journal* 53: 834–857.

Wunnava, P.V. and J.R. Henley. 1987. "Pooled Cross-Section Time-Series Examination of the Effects of Unemployment Insurance Compensation on Unemployment Rate and Unemployment Duration," *Economics Letters* 25: 367–371.

INDEX